DICKENS AND ELLEN TERNAN

*I hope that my books will speak
for themselves and me, when I and
my faults and virtues, my fortunes
and misfortunes are all forgotten.*
Letter of CHARLES DICKENS

Dickens & Ellen Ternan

BY
ADA NISBET
WITH A FOREWORD BY
EDMUND WILSON

1952
UNIVERSITY OF CALIFORNIA PRESS
BERKELEY AND LOS ANGELES

UNIVERSITY OF CALIFORNIA PRESS
BERKELEY AND LOS ANGELES, CALIFORNIA

CAMBRIDGE UNIVERSITY PRESS
LONDON, ENGLAND

COPYRIGHT, 1952, BY
THE REGENTS OF THE UNIVERSITY OF CALIFORNIA

PRINTED IN THE UNITED STATES OF AMERICA

DESIGNED BY JOHN B. GOETZ

FOR

Bessie

THIS LITTLE HANGOUT

AFTER A BIG WASH

Foreword

THERE IS something more to our interest in the private lives of great men than the mere desire to pry into other people's personal affairs. A great writer, for example, represents a special concentration both of purpose and of sensibility. He is more conscious than other people of the things that are going on in his time, and he is more articulate about them. He is driven to formulate more clearly some attitude toward the world that he lives in. But the works that he gives to the public do not tell the whole of his story, for they must always be artificial arrangements in the interests of ideal values. The real struggle of the ideal with the actual can only be seen at close range in the relationships and vicissitudes of the man's own life. The more intimate of these relationships, the less edifying of these vicissitudes, can usually not be explored until after the man is dead, and the feelings of his family or friends as well as respect for the current conventions sometimes operate to prevent them from being made public till a very long time after; but when there is no longer anyone left to be hurt or embarrassed by them, such documents as survive may legitimately be put at the disposal of anybody interested in the subject. Even though these may seem to show the great man in an unpleasant or discreditable light, his reputation, if his work has stood up, cannot seriously be injured by them; and they are likely to afford insights of

vii

a kind that we cannot get in any other way into the lives of the beings who have gone before us.

There may of course be a conflict of interest, when the attempt at revelation is premature, between the public who want to find out and the family who want to conceal —the kind of situation so amusingly dramatized by Henry James in *The Aspern Papers;* and in the case of Charles Dickens, such a conflict has lasted longer than is normal, because family loyalty to Dickens has been extended in a special way by a body of old-fashioned Dickensians who, even after Dickens's descendants have authorized publication of the facts about his later life, have persistently continued to oppose it, either because they regard it as a duty to keep up the Victorian pretenses or because they are themselves so naïve that they cannot believe the truth. That Dickens put away his wife for a young actress named Ellen Ternan was well known to his closest friends and long provided a subject of gossip in literary London; but, though mentioned several times in the press and in the memoirs of various contemporaries, this affair was not dealt with at length in any biography of Dickens till, in 1936, the late Thomas Wright published his *Life of Charles Dickens.* This book was followed three years later by Gladys Storey's *Dickens and Daughter,* a report of conversations with Kate Perugini, Dickens's younger daughter, who had given Mrs. Storey a full account of the Ellen Ternan episode and requested her eventually to publish it. The reliability of this account was vouched for at the time by Bernard Shaw, who had known Mrs. Perugini. It may seem strange, then, that the old-fashioned Dickens-lovers should still shrink from accepting this testimony and continue to imagine as a model of sound middle-class character a man so relentlessly harrowed by violent internal conflicts as Dickens seems plainly to have been and so notoriously unhappy in his domestic life, who had been brought by his worldly success as well as by his devastating genius as a critic of institutions to a position where there was little to deter him from gratifying his inclinations. Yet they have tried, as Miss Nisbet here shows, to explain away both Wright and Miss Storey, and they have consistently denounced all the writers on Dickens who have accepted the love affair with Ellen Ternan as mischievous calumniators of a great and good man.

Now, Charles Dickens was indeed a great man, one of the top geniuses of the nineteenth century, and the events of his emotional life, however disconcerting they may prove, should be treated with a respect as scrupulous as that which has been brought to those of a Wagner's or a Dostoevsky's. Miss Ada Nisbet, who has been working on a study of Dickens's relations with America and who is one of the board of advisory editors of the definitive edition of Dickens's letters now in progress, became interested in the problem of Ellen Ternan, whom she found turning up in various connections which had not before been noticed. Her findings she presents in this book, which includes some entirely new documents as well as others that had not been collected. Miss Nisbet is able to show that, even apart from Miss Storey and Wright, there are very strong indications that Dickens set up Ellen Ternan in an establishment of her own, that he traveled with her both in England and on the Continent, and that he had even thought of bringing her to the United States when he came here on a reading tour. By applying infrared rays to a series of canceled passages in Dickens's letters, at the time of this tour, to his assistant on the magazine he edited, she has discovered that Dickens wrote regularly to Ellen under cover of this correspondence and referred to her in terms that seem warmer than those of mere affectionate friendship. The statement made by Wright that Dickens had children or a child by Ellen is not supported by independent evidence; but the unprejudiced reader of Miss Nisbet's book will certainly come to the conclusion that, if Dickens's relations with Ellen were, as the Dickensians insist, Platonic, he was an even odder case than one had thought. In this connection, I should like to suggest that the resounding vindication by Dickens, in the second of the statements he published at the time of his separation from his wife, of the purity of "a young lady" who was evidently Ellen Ternan may—if Dickens was not merely lying like a gentleman—be explained on the ground that the liaison did not really begin until after the situation had been cleared up by the formal separation and Ellen had been established on a kind of official basis.

The personality of Ellen Ternan evidently plays an important role in Dickens's later works. Thomas Wright pointed out that the names of Dickens's last three heroines —Estella Provis, Bella Wilfer, and Helena Landless—must all be derived from hers: her full name was Ellen Lawless Ternan; and their relations with their masculine vis-à-vis seem all to be based on phases of Dickens's relations with Ellen. She brought a new motif into Dickens's work, though this has a certain kinship with older motifs. He seems to have been first attracted to her when he found her weeping behind the scenes because she had to appear on the stage in what she felt to be an immodest costume, and she must have appealed to him in the character—which

had played such a part in his books—of the innocent
suffering child. Yet in his later novels the women in-
spired by Ellen combine in various ways three other of
Dickens's recurrent types: the little coquette, the proud
lady and the ferocious implacable shrew. What these heroines all have in common is summed up by Thomas Wright
as follows: "All three ladies were very pretty, all were
proud, acting like spoiled children, petulant, difficult to
manage and capricious. All were gifted, and each rose
from straitened circumstances to a higher position.
Estella Provis married Bentley Drummle, who has nothing to recommend him but his purse. Bella Wilfer said,
'I must have money, Pa, I must marry it'; and Helena
Landless apparently meant to have Lieutenant Tartar
of the Royal Navy, who had come into possession of a
fortune." These young women are perhaps more attractive than any of his other heroines. Yet the relations between Pip and Estella are negative: he adores her and she
likes to torture him; those between Rokesmith and Bella,
though a great show of gaiety is made, are not really
very exhilarating; and it is impossible to tell what role
the boyish Helena Landless is to play in the unfinished
Edwin Drood. In the somber later novels of Dickens,
these heroines cannot be unaffected by the atmosphere
in which they move. And everything that we hear about
Dickens and Ellen seems, on both sides, humiliating
and painful. It is a pity that we should know so little—
apart from these characters that carry her name—about
Ellen's real personality and her attitude toward her lover.
Thomas Wright says that he was told by a Canon Benham
who was something of an authority on Dickens that she
"continued, after Dickens's death, to brood over her con-

nection with him. At last she disburdened her mind to Canon Benham. She told him the whole story and declared that she loathed the very thought of this intimacy." She was eventually to marry a clergyman. One gets an impression that she was commonplace, not very imaginative or sensitive and not very much interested in Dickens, and that she figured not only uncomfortably but perhaps even uncomprehendingly in the dramas with which Dickens was peopling the imaginative life of the world but which probably left him still without human contacts. Yet one of Ellen's sisters wrote novels and married a brother of Trollope's, and the other painted and wrote and had apparently some talent as an actress, so Ellen, whom we know less, may not have been so bad as that.

EDMUND WILSON

Preface

THIS small volume is a by-product. For ten years, in the course of gathering materials for a book on Dickens and America, I have been rummaging through unpublished letters, old diaries and memoirs, and nineteenth-century newspapers and periodicals. Inevitably I ran across a great deal more about Dickens than was directly pertinent to my specific project. Since much of this material was completely new and threw light upon aspects of Dickens's life and character that had been left unexplored by most of his biographers, I found myself taking notes so that my understanding of Dickens's relations with America would be enlarged by a deeper and truer knowledge of Dickens himself.

These notes would probably have remained unpublished, except as they might have found a place in the larger study now in progress, if it had not been for the violence of certain recent attacks upon the reliability and integrity of those critics and scholars who have accepted the story of Dickens's liaison with Ellen Ternan as fact. The attackers claim there is no "evidence." I have gathered an accumulation of what I am convinced constitutes "evidence." I respect the critics and writers under fire, who include such people as Dame Una Pope-Hennessy, Hesketh Pearson, Edmund Wilson, Lionel Stevenson, Clifton Fadiman, and W. Somerset Maugham among others, and

I resent the nature and tone of the attacks. This volume is the result.

My grateful thanks go to the John Simon Guggenheim Foundation, the American Association of University Women, and the Research Committee of the University of California, who by their generous support, at various times during the past ten years, of my work in the field of Anglo-American relations have also supported, however unwittingly, this fledgling by-product.

I wish also to thank Mr. Henry Charles Dickens, present holder of the Dickens copyrights, for his permission to publish those letters and parts of letters that appear here in print for the first time. I feel that Mr. Dickens cannot be too warmly commended for his sane and enlightened attitude toward the scholarly use of the private papers of such an important public figure as Charles Dickens.

Permission to reproduce or to quote from unpublished manuscripts in their collections has also been granted by the following: The Huntington Library, San Marino, California; the Henry W. and Albert A. Berg Collection of the New York Public Library; the Trustees of the Pierpont Morgan Library, New York; and the Massachusetts Historical Society, Boston. I wish to express my appreciation for these permissions as well as for the generous coöperation and help given me by the staffs of these libraries, especially by Dr. John D. Gordan, Dr. Frederick B. Adams, Jr., and Mr. Herbert C. Schulz. I wish also to acknowledge the permission to publish George Bernard Shaw's letter to the editor of the *Times* Literary Supplement of July 29, 1939, granted by the Society of Authors and the Public Trustee. For permission to quote at length from the Nonesuch edition of Dickens's letters I am indebted to the generosity of Rupert Hart-Davis, Ltd., who, as publishers of the new edition of the letters of Charles Dickens now in progress, have acquired the Nonesuch copyright.

I am indebted to Miss Gladys Storey for her helpful answers to a number of inquiries, and for permission to quote from her book, *Dickens and Daughter,* as well as from some of her personal letters to me. Another English friend and scholar, Mr. Kenneth J. Fielding, has been of invaluable assistance in checking on materials in England and in calling my attention to a number of obscure items. Mr. G. W. Nash, director of the Enthoven Theatre Collection of the Victoria and Albert Museum, London, and Mr. A. V. Hull, Superintendent of the British Museum Newspaper Library, have given generous aid on special problems. I am grateful to Professor James Lee Harlan of the Colorado Agricultural and Mechanical College for sharing with me his special and extensive knowledge of John Forster's relations with Dickens. To Professor Morton D. Zabel of the University of Chicago and to Mr. Edmund Wilson, both of whom were kind enough to read the manuscript, I am indebted for many helpful critical suggestions and advice.

A special note of appreciation goes to my colleague, Professor Franklin P. Rolfe, who was the first to work on the Dickens materials in the Huntington Library, but who generously turned over his notes for my use and gave valuable assistance with difficult transcriptions of manuscripts. Many other colleagues have assisted by their criticisms of the manuscript, publication of which has certainly been hastened by their exhortations, cajolings, and encourage-

ment; to acknowledge all such indebtedness would be to
make public my Christmas-card list. I thank them all, as I
thank Mr. Glenn Gosling of the University of California
Press, for their help, their encouragement, and for their
patient endurance.

Finally, I thank Louis B. Wright, who started all this
by asking me, back in 1948, to read a paper at the Folger
Shakespeare Library.   A. N.

Contents

1
Household Saint

WHEN Charles Dickens died in 1870, the press was filled with the most extravagant panegyric. Women wept in flowered sonnets. Editor outpurpled editor; "Wherever the English tongue is spoken," lyricized one, "—amid the endless pine forests of Canada, the luxuriant pastures of Australia, or the sun-scorched plains of India—will the news fall like a heavy blow." [1] And his fellow journalists, dusting off their thesauri, followed suit. Two Deans of the Church of England argued over whether Dickens should be buried at Rochester Cathedral or in Westminster Abbey. Many years later William Michael Rossetti put it down as a matter of serious record that two events interrupted the successful sale of his brother's new edition of poems in 1870—the outbreak of the Franco-Prussian War and the death of Dickens.[2] Many business houses closed shop the day after the news was announced. Flags flew at half-mast. Placards edged in black hung in the railway stations.

Some, it is true, balked at this swinging of censers. The London *Literary World* deprecated "eulogies almost idolatrous," [3] and in Boston the quarrel that took place among the clergymen of different sects became a national scandal. An evangelical minister objected that on the Sunday following the announcement of Dickens's death "every Unitarian and Universalist pulpit in Boston sent

For numbered notes, see pages 75–89 below.

1

him to heaven immediately."⁴ One pious orator, in a
sermon which was published and circulated throughout
the country, envisioned the novelist as he wrote of Little
Nell, "holy as a surpliced priest," and apostrophized
Dickens in the words: "Farewell, gentle spirit. . . .
Thy freed spirit walks in glory."⁵ The Rev. Justin D. Fulton, a Baptist minister, delivered an answering sermon
protesting in strong terms what he called "the canonization
of Charles Dickens,"⁶ a sermon which set off repercussions
in the entire American press. Fulton was branded a narrow-
minded, backbiting vilifier by an aroused public, and
clergymen of all sects joined in the quarrel. A fellow Baptist, commending Fulton's courage, ·went on to say:
"When Mr. Dickens is eulogized as the brightest name in
English literature since Shakespeare, we can smile at the
simplicity of such a judgment; when he is spoken of as the
greatest moral reformer and benefactor of his time, we
can pardon something to the enthusiasm of those who have
been charmed by his humor or subdued by his pathos; but
when he is presented to us as the exemplary Christian, and
it is declared that his death freed him from his last im-
perfection and ushered him into everlasting bliss, it is
needful for some one to protest."⁷

But in the end the canonizers had their way. The
shrine was erected. The veil was drawn. Voices dropped
to a reverent hush.

In the eighty years since his death, the Dickensian
cult has grown to such proportions that to find any fault
in Dickens is, as was once remarked of Longfellow, like
carrying a rifle into a national park—though with Dickens
it is an international park. Hardly another figure of history
has been surrounded by such an aura of intense personal

devotion. Surely no other author can claim so many repro-
ductions—graphic, plastic, ceramic, cinematic—of his crea-
tions, so many books devoted to his inns, his streets, his
schools, his prisons, his child characters, his doctors, his
lawyers, his clergymen. You can subscribe to a monthly
magazine devoted entirely to Dickens; you can paper your
den with scenes from *Pickwick,* eat your salad from a
Copperfield plate, and drink your beer from a Micawber
mug. You can even shake your salt and pepper out of
Pumblechook or Sairey Gamp, and flick your ashes into
Oliver's gruel bowl. All these are tributes to the creative
genius of a great writer and are wholly unobjectionable.
The world would be poorer without them, as would the
world's language without their originals. Certainly any
of today's young people who meet with blank incompre-
hension such terms as "Podsnappian," "Pecksniffian,"
"Micawberism," or "Mrs. Leo Hunter" have been linguis-
tically disfranchised by their parents and educators.

Unobjectionable as such sentimental tributes may be,
however, they add little to a real appreciation of Dickens's
genius. Such appreciation can come only from a careful
study of his novels, combined with an equally careful study
of the man Dickens as distinguished from the writer and
especially as dissociated from the legend. It is a natural
error on the part of readers to ascribe to the writer himself the virtues he extols in his writings. Certainly it
has been a common error with Dickensians. Dickens's
heroes are usually kind, generous, benevolent men, who
shrink from all the vices and practice all the virtues; ergo,
Dickens himself was a man incapable of the smallest vice.
Above all, Dickens had celebrated domestic virtue, and
so he was enshrined as a special kind of household saint.

Not many have bothered to disbelieve the Byron or
Shelley scandals. The discovery of Wordsworth's Annette
caused only a ripple of surprise and little pious objection.
In their own day John Stuart Mill and George Eliot faced
up to criticism and were uninjured by it. The private lives
of Bulwer-Lytton and Wilkie Collins were so well known
as to be of little interest to gossips. Parnell's relations with
Mrs. O'Shea were common knowledge for a long time
before his political enemies used them as a means of break-
ing him. But it has been different with Dickens. From the
beginning, rumors faded away because they were invari-
ably disbelieved. The test was always: "Could the creator
of Little Nell have done such a thing?" or "Could such
a man have written *A Christmas Carol?*" And the rumor
withered into extinction because only unfeeling brutes
who were capable of knocking Tiny Tim's crutches out
from under him would have repeated it.

As the Catholic Church has discovered, however, it
is best not to be in a hurry about canonization proceedings.
The years have a quiet way of sifting out the truth, and
undeserved laurels fall into the dust along with undeserved
calumnies. In recent years facts, not rumors, have been
knocking at the wall that Victorian reticence built around
the man Dickens. Unfortunately, the gradual disclosure
of these facts has led to irresponsible name calling both by
overreverent Dickensians and by certain Dickens biographers. Nothing is gained by damning the Dickens legend
as "the Dickensian Lie," as was done by Mr. Jack Lindsay, a recent biographer.[8] Nor do Dickensians like Mr.
Edward Wagenknecht gain anything when they greet
each unwelcome discovery as a slander or brand the

scholars and biographers who make these discoveries "peeping Toms," "ghouls," and "scandalmongers." [9] Biography is not hagiography, and English biography ("Bless its mealy mouth!" as Carlyle once exclaimed) no longer countenances distortions or suppressions where its really great figures are concerned. The biographer must be allowed to pursue fact as freely as the historian or scientist, and no one should condemn him because in his search for truth he sometimes finds it.

Actually, Dickens was far more complex and interesting than the two-dimensional emasculated figure that emerges from the pietistic studies crowding library shelves. The reader may not *like* the real Dickens as much as the legendary one, but likes or dislikes have little relation to the satisfaction that comes from an understanding and knowledge of such a man as Dickens. Those who want only to like him, as William Dean Howells once remarked, "can always escape from his life to his works." [10]

The chief objection of the extreme Dickensians has been that biographers and critics offer insufficient evidence for certain recent revelations. And of course the key "evidence" they are talking about concerns whether or not the obscure actress Ellen Lawless Ternan was Dickens's mistress during the last twelve years of his life. In his lifetime the majority of Dickens's public accepted his own explanation of "temperamental incompatibility" as the cause of his separation, in 1858, from the mother of his ten children. Since his death most Dickensians have met each new outcropping of the rumor about the novelist's interest in the eighteen-year-old Ellen with the same outraged protestations with which Dickens himself met such charges at the time of the separation. Certainly the time has come for an honest review of the whole matter, presenting what evidence there is and letting the case rest upon it.

It is undeniable that Dickens's family and close friends did suppress the facts, and that the Dickens cult has chosen to ignore or deny every least suggestion regarding Ellen Ternan's relation to Dickens. On the other hand, the Dickensians are right in their charge that few biographers or critics in recent years have done much original research, but have gone on repeating each other with unquestioning acceptance of often undocumented statements. The late Dame Una Pope-Hennessy, writing her biography in 1946, was the first to use materials brought together in the three-volume Nonesuch edition of Dickens's letters, published in 1938; but she did not go to original manuscripts, and the Nonesuch, valuable as it is, is incomplete and often inaccurate. Nor do Dickens's most recent biographers, Mr. Hesketh Pearson, Mr. Jack Lindsay, or Mr. Julian Symons, appear to have gone to original manuscripts.

In the mass of unpublished and incompletely published Dickens letters, several thousand of which are now in this country in the important collections at the Henry E. Huntington, New York Public, and Pierpont Morgan libraries, there is enough fresh material for a substantial reinterpretation of Dickens, both as man and as artist. All this awaits the new biographer of Dickens. In the meantime it would seem that such information as these letters afford on the Ternan affair should be given to the public in the interest of putting a stop both to backstairs gossip and to irresponsible attacks upon the integrity of the many reputable writers and scholars who have assumed the truth of the story.

The purpose here is to review the entire history of the Dickens-Ternan relationship: first, the facts that have been known and generally accepted; then the statements that have seeped into print as gossip or rumor over the years; and finally, the entirely new "evidence" contained in heretofore unpublished letters, which will lend the strong support of Dickens's personal testimony to the accumulation of reports of his love for the young actress Ellen Ternan.

There is no intention of debunking in this presentation. The strong currents of pathos and tragedy that run throughout the history of the affair prompt a very different mood in the thoughtful reader. The only intention is to present the facts and to urge the acceptance of those facts. Dickens is too great a figure to continue the victim of suppression and distortion at whatever loving and well-meaning hands. Mr. T. W. Hill, an ardent Dickensian, has remarked that "all that is required is reasonable substantiation of statements. Give us substantiation and the facts must be accepted at once." [11] Here, then, is that substantiation—in the incontrovertible hand of Dickens himself.

2

Ellen Ternan

CERTAIN FACTS about Ellen Lawless Ternan are a matter of record. She was a daughter of Frances Eleanor and Thomas Lawless Ternan, both of the theater. Mrs. Ternan, as Fanny Jarman, made her first appearance on the stage with her mother at the age of twelve, and before she was sixteen had become a leading lady at the Bath Theatre. She was well known in the lesser theatricals of her time, appearing with Charles Kemble and Charles Kean among others, and receiving praise from such critics as Hazlitt, Leigh Hunt, and Christopher North. In 1834 she was married to Thomas Ternan and they left immediately for a three years' tour of America, from Quebec to New Orleans. In Montreal they played at the Theatre Royal, the very theater where, in 1842, Dickens and his wife took part in an amateur performance. Contemporary records reveal that the Ternans' reception in America was unenthusiastic, though Joseph Ireland could write of "Miss Jarman" that "rarely has so cultivated a mind been united with such an agreeable and elegant exterior." [1] New Yorkers resented their opening in Philadelphia instead of New York, and Philadelphians objected to Tom Ternan's appearance as a wigless, bald-headed Romeo. [2] Not much more is known of Ternan except that he was a Dublin actor-manager who reputedly committed suicide in an insane asylum in 1846. [3]

8

His death left Mrs. Ternan with three little girls, Frances Eleanor, Maria, and Ellen Lawless, all of whom went on the stage at an early age. The English actor Macready, who had known and acted with Tom Ternan (whom he once described as "opinionated, jealous, and . . . little-minded"),[4] was moved by the tragedy of his death and offered financial assistance to Mrs. Ternan, then playing opposite him in *The Merchant of Venice*. He describes in his diary how "Poor Mrs. Ternan was much affected in reciting the *beautiful* speech on mercy (has the Bible anything better?), and she made a woman of me. She brought her three little girls to see me, and her mother came after. Poor thing. She appears very grateful for a little act of duty." [5] Mrs. Ternan seems to have quit the stage about 1857 or 1858, except for a performance of blind Alice in *The Bride of Lammermoor* with Charles Fechter in 1866. She died at the home of her daughter Maria on October 30, 1873.

In a diary entry for 1845 Macready speaks of sending for Mrs. Ternan and asking to see "her little gifted girl." [6] This was probably Maria, who appears to have been the most talented actress of the three sisters. Playbills of the Drury Lane, Royal Olympic, and Haymarket theaters of the 1850's and 1860's list her name in a great number of varied parts. Dickens himself wrote of Maria: "I remember her on the stage, a little child, and I daresay she was born in a country theatre." [7] At another time he spoke of her as "born on the stage and inured to it from the days when she was the little child in Pizarro." [8] A number of his letters urge theatrical friends to give parts to Maria or to Mrs. Ternan, and other letters contain rhapsodic descriptions of Maria's acting.[9] Later in her life, after her marriage to

W. Rowland Taylor, she attained some distinction as an artist and portrait painter,[10] and, during a residence in Rome, served for some years as a special correspondent for the London *Standard*.

Frances Eleanor Ternan, the eldest daughter, was born in Philadelphia on August 17, 1835, when the Ternans were in America. At seven years old she made her first appearance at the Strand Theatre, but her later theatrical career was undistinguished and she abandoned it in 1856.[11] She had a pleasant singing voice and seems to have had aspirations toward a musical career. In 1866 she was married to Anthony Trollope's widowed brother, Thomas Adolphus Trollope, a man twenty-five years her senior. She had met Trollope when studying voice in Italy, through a letter of introduction from Dickens to Trollope's mother, the famous author of *Domestic Manners of the Americans*.[12] When Thomas Adolphus' first wife died in 1865, it was arranged that Frances Eleanor should come to his villa in Florence as a companion to his young daughter. Within two months Tom and "Fanny" were engaged, and three months later they were married. Anthony Trollope, who knew and admired Frances, is credited by his brother in his autobiography, *What I Remember*, with having urged the marriage, which took place in Paris so that Mrs. Ternan, Maria (then Mrs. W. Rowland Taylor), and Anthony and his wife could more conveniently attend.[13]

The "Italian Trollopes," as they were known to distinguish them from the Anthony Trollopes, were intimate with many well-known figures of the time, especially the Brownings and the Alfred Austins. In his autobiography Austin writes enthusiastically of Frances at the time she first came to the Villa Trollope, praising her singing and speaking of her love of walking and picnicking. "Though thoroughly feminine in every respect," he records, she "had an almost masculine mind in the sphere of serious intellectual deliberation." [14] While at Florence and just before her marriage, Francis got her start in what was to prove a fairly successful literary career by the publication of her first two novels, *Aunt Margaret's Trouble* and *Mabel's Progress,* in the pages of Dickens's magazine, *All the Year Round.*[15] Her best-known work among a long list of minor novels, biographies, translations, travel accounts, and studies of music, art, and literature is probably the biography of her famous mother-in-law, Frances Milton Trollope.[16]

Ellen Lawless Ternan was born the same year as Dickens's younger daughter Kate, on March 3, 1839. Though apparently not so talented as her mother or sister Maria, she was a member with them of Charles Kean's Shakespeare company at the Princess Theatre, and appeared in various parts at the Olympic and Haymarket theaters in the 1850's.[17] At one of these appearances, when she was playing the part of Hippomenes in Francis Talfourd's *Atalanta,* on April 14, 1857, Dickens is said to have gone backstage before curtain time, where he came upon the eighteen-year-old actress in tears over having to wear an overscanty costume. This may have been the novelist's first meeting with Ellen.[18] A contemporary notice of her performance in *Atalanta* describes her as "a debutante with a pretty face and well-developed figure, who when she had gained more confidence would become an acquisition." [19] In 1876, six years after the death of Dickens, Ellen Ternan married an Anglican clergyman, the Rev. George Wharton

Robinson, who later gave up orders and became headmaster of his own school at Margate. Ellen died in 1914.

Certain facts about Ellen's connection with Dickens are common knowledge. In 1856, Dickens collaborated with Wilkie Collins in the writing of a play, *The Frozen Deep*, for an amateur performance to be given by Dickens and his family and friends at his own home. After the success of the first performance, on January 8, 1857, it was decided to give several public performances for the benefit of the recently bereaved family of Douglas Jerrold, one of which performances the Queen and Prince Consort attended. When plans developed for the play to be given in Manchester in August of 1857, Dickens wrote to Wilkie Collins, "It [the theater] is *an immense place,* and we shall be obliged to have actresses. . . . (I am already trying to get the best who *have been* on the stage.)" [20] The best included Mrs. Ternan and her two daughters Maria and Ellen, who replaced the amateur actresses.

Less than a year later, on June 12, 1858, Dickens announced to a startled public, in a long statement headed "PERSONAL" appearing in the front pages of his magazine, *Household Words,*[21] that he was separating from the mother of his ten children (nine then living) after twenty-two years of marriage. The eldest son, Charles, Jr., aged 21, went with his mother.[22] The next oldest boy, aged 17, had just been sent off to service in India. Dickens kept the girls, aged 19 and 18, and the five younger boys, aged 13, 12, 10, 8, and 6. Georgina Hogarth, Mrs. Dickens's unmarried younger sister, who had been living with the Dickenses for fifteen years, remained in the Dickens household as a kind of housekeeper, foster mother, and social hostess. For many years she did not see or speak to her sister, her mother, or the rest of her family.[23]

Rumors of all sorts naturally abounded. In the middle of Victoria's reign, the "putting away" of one's wife, which is what the separation amounted to, leaving eight underage children motherless (except for an anomalous sister-in-law), was an almost unprecedented action. Dickens's protestations of simple incompatibility, familiar enough today, were incomprehensible to the Victorian public. A man did not break up his home and risk his reputation as the celebrator of domestic virtue just because he no longer "got on" with his wife. Contemporaries, many of whom had no notion of separating from wives they did not get on with, looked for deeper reasons, and, in the gentlemanly, circumspect, typically English way, rumors began to circulate. No one printed an outright attack, though there were some veiled hints. But people talked and wrote letters as the bones rattled in the Gad's Hill closets.

Many looked askance at Georgina Hogarth, a natural target for the uninformed, but those closer to Dickens talked about an actress called "Nelly." And almost everyone, whether believing the stories that were in circulation or not, condemned Dickens's action. Elizabeth Barrett Browning wrote a friend, "What is this sad story about Dickens & his wife? Incompatibility of temper after twenty-three years of married life? What a plea!—Worse than irregularity of the passions, it seems to me. Thinking of my own peace & selfish pleasure, too, I would rather be beaten by my husband once a day than lose my child out of the house—yes, indeed. And the Dickens's have children younger than Penini!—Poor woman! She must suffer bit-terly—that is sure." [24] Mrs. Browning's sentiments were echoed by Thackeray, who wrote his mother, "To think of the poor matron after 22 years of marriage going away out of her house! O dear me its a fatal story for our trade." [25]

The irony is that perhaps little would be known of the gossip today if Dickens had not made it a matter of record by his widespread denials. No more than a handful of people could have heard the Ternan stories. But when Dickens, determined to quash the rumors, asked the leading periodicals of England and America to reprint his personal statement from *Household Words* denying them, he scattered the gossip across the globe. In this statement he declared that "all the lately whispered rumours touching the trouble at which I have glanced are abominably false. And . . . whosoever repeats one of them, after this denial, will lie as wilfully and as foully as it is possible for any false witness to lie, before heaven and earth." [26] It was a step which, according to his intimate friend Edmund Yates, "did him more harm than the separation itself." [27] John Forster records in his biography of Dickens that he urged the novelist not to publish the statement, but Dickens preferred to follow the advice of "a certain distinguished man" (i.e., John Delane, editor of the *Times*).[28] Criticisms of his action in dragging his private affairs before the public began pouring in. "He has quite spoilt our taste for that greatest of all the Dickens fictions—himself," wryly observed a contributor in the periodical *John Bull*. . . . "People will feel that they have been humbugged out of their idolatry." [29] More and more expressions of sympathy with Mrs. Dickens found their way into print.

Then a second statement appeared in all the leading papers, even more shocking to the public than the first.

Dickens had included this statement in a letter to his friend
Arthur Smith, begging him to circulate its contents in
rebuttal of the slanders against him. In it Dickens attempted
to protect himself by launching an attack upon Mrs.
Dickens. Among other ungenerous statements, Dickens
announced that his wife suffered from a "mental disorder"
and that the "peculiarity of her character has thrown all the
children on some one else." The "some one else" was,
of course, Georgina Hogarth, of whom Dickens wrote:
"From the age of fifteen she has devoted herself to our
house and our children. . . . I do not know—I cannot by
any stretch of fancy imagine—what would have become of
them but for this aunt, who has grown up with them, to
whom they are devoted, and who has sacrificed the best
part of her youth and life to them. . . . [She] has a
higher claim . . . upon my affection, respect and gratitude than anybody in this world." Dickens had preceded
these remarks by writing, "In the manly consideration
towards Mrs. Dickens which I owe my wife," upon which
the Liverpool *Mercury* commented, "If this is 'manly consideration,' we should like to be favoured with a definition
of unmanly selfishness and heartlessness." [30]

This second statement went on to say: "Two wicked
persons, who should have spoken very differently of me
in consideration of earned respect and gratitude, have . . .
coupled with this separation the name of a young lady
for whom I have great attachment and regard. I will not
repeat her name—I honour it too much. Upon my soul
and honour, there is not on this earth a more virtuous and
spotless creature than that young lady. I know her to be
innocent and pure, and as good as my own dear daughters."
The "two wicked persons" were his wife's mother and

youngest sister, from whom Dickens had somehow obtained a signed recantation.[31] The statement and appended recantation were dated May 29, 1858, but were first published in the New York *Tribune* on August 16, 1858. Both were copied, as was the custom of the time, by most of the journals of England and America.

The clamor against Dickens for making such public accusations, whether true or not, was so violent that Dickens hastened to disclaim any responsibility for the publication, which, he said, was a violation of confidence. Since then the document has always been referred to as "the violated letter." However, it was not a "letter," but a statement handed over to a man who was the manager of his public readings, a kind of public-relations agent. And attached to the statement was a note which read: "My dear Arthur—You have not only my full permission to show this, but I beg of you to show it to any one who wishes to do me right, or to any one who may have been misled into doing me wrong." Furthermore, Dickens never wavered in his friendship for the "violator." Smith, once described by Edmund Yates as "a timid man by nature,"[32] continued in his position as secretary and manager of the readings; in fact, in November, 1858, Dickens wrote George Dolby's daughter (Dolby was later to become Dickens's manager), "I have not, I assure you, the remotest idea of severing myself from Arthur Smith,"[33] which would indicate that others thought he would surely dismiss the "violator." At Smith's death three years later, Dickens wrote, "It is as if my right arm were gone," and spoke of the "wonderful tact and consummate mastery of arrangement"[34] of the man whose blunder distributed the "violated" one's dirtiest linen throughout two continents. It is difficult to avoid the suspicion that the blunder was Dickens's, not Arthur Smith's.

Certainly when lesser crimes were committed against his interests Dickens exhibited no such sense of loyalty. When his publishers Bradbury and Evans declined to run his first separation statement in the pages of *Punch*, Dickens took offense, broke his publishing relations with them, resigned his editorship of their magazine, *Household Words*, and set up his own magazine, which he named *All the Year Round* after Forster raised understandable objections to his first choice, "Household Harmony." Three years later, Dickens refused to attend his eldest son's marriage to Evans's daughter and declared flatly that he would never enter their home. When Mark Lemon, editor of *Punch* and one of Dickens's closest personal friends for many years, became Mrs. Dickens's representative in the separation proceedings, Dickens broke the friendship to the point of forbidding the children to speak to "Uncle Mark," as they were forbidden to see or speak to their grandmother or Aunt Helen, Mrs. Dickens's mother and sister.[35]

For Dickens, the separation became a crucial test of all his friendships. Those who so much as asked Mrs. Dickens to dine after the separation sacrificed the friendship of her separated husband. Those who took his side, as did the young actress Mary Boyle in effusive letters of sympathy,[36] or Edmund Yates in his column in *Town Talk*,[37] were bound to Dickens with hoops of steel. There is little doubt that Dickens's partisan support of Yates against Thackeray in their famous controversy was tied in with his sense of gratitude to Yates and his anger over what he thought was Thackeray's alignment against him in this

crisis. Explaining to Thackeray why he agreed to represent Yates, in a letter which Dickens suggested Thackeray
burn after reading it, Dickens wrote that Yates had
"recently done me a manly service I can never forget, in
some private distress of mind (generally within your
knowledge) and he naturally thought of me as his friend
in an emergency." [38]

Thackeray wrote his mother at the time of the separation: "Here is sad news in the literary world—no less than
a separation between M^r & Mrs Dickens—with all sorts
of horrible stories buzzing about. The worst is that Im in a
manner dragged in for one—Last week going into the
Garrick I heard that D is separated from his wife on account of an intrigue with his sister in law. No says I no
such thing—its with an actress—and the other story has not
got to Dickens's ears but this has—and he fancies that I
am going about abusing him! We shall never be allowed
to be friends that's clear. I had mine from a man at Epsom
the first I ever heard of the matter, and should have said
nothing about it but that I heard the other much worse
story whereupon I told mine to counteract it. There is
some row about an actress in the case, & he denies with
the utmost infuriation any charge against her or himself.
. . . I havent seen the statement but this is what is
brought to me on my bed of sickness, and I'd give 100 £
[if it weren't true]." [39] Thackeray's later kindness to Mrs.
Dickens was probably another source of irritation to his
rival novelist. All this extreme touchiness on the matter of
the separation, especially since Mrs. Dickens herself maintained a dignified silence (Dickens should have been
married to that notorious shrew, Rosina Bulwer-Lytton!),
does not argue in favor of Dickens's explanation that in-

compatibility was the sole cause of his domestic difficulties; if so, surely the separated wife could be permitted to see old friends with no injury to the husband.[40]

Neither of the separation statements mentions Ellen Ternan by name. Some have felt that Dickens was defending Georgina only, and it is probably true that her name and reputation were part of his defense;[41] he may even have emphasized her innocence, as he certainly does, to direct attention away from Ellen. But he does mention in the first statement that "innocent persons" were involved in the rumors, so that more than one must have been named in them. Also, it is unlikely that the person whom Dickens accused his mother-in-law and sister-in-law of libeling would have been their own daughter and sister, Georgina. This supposition is upheld in a suppressed passage of a letter now in the Morgan Library. Addressed to his actor friend, William Charles Macready, and dated June 7, 1858, the very day of the appearance of the first "statement" in the pages of the *Times*, it gives Dickens's reasons for publishing the statement: "The question was not I myself; but others. Foremost among them—of all people in the world—Georgina! Mrs. Dickens's weakness, and her mother's and her youngest sister's wickedness, drifted to that, without seeing what they would strike against—though I warned them in the strongest manner." Also, Dickens made it clear in the many letters he set in motion at this time, as part of a campaign of self-defense, that the rumors centered on someone other than Georgina. As Thackeray wrote a friend: "I have a note from Mr. Dickens on the subject of a common report derogatory to the honor of a young lady whose name has been mentioned in connection with his. He authorizes me to contradict the

rumour on his own solemn word and his wife's authority." [42]

Furthermore, there is substantiating evidence in many
of the newspaper comments of the time that Ellen's name
was being linked with Dickens's. The London correspondent of the New York *Times* wrote at the time of the
separation: "All London, you must know, had for some
time been rife with legends concerning Dickens and an actress, with whom it was at last affirmed that the author
of David Copperfield had eloped to Boulogne." [43] True,
most such reports were immediately followed by statements
of emphatic disbelief; the *Times* correspondent went on to
say that the rumor was a "lying scandal which should be
scotched or the many whose faith in the wholesome lessons
of Pickwick, Master Humphrey's Clock, and the Christmas
Stories might also be shaken in the author's failure to
achieve in his own life the ideas of peace and harmony
which he has painted." But the rumors continued to circulate. The epithet "a meritorious young actress" soon
became the favored designation in press accounts of the
separation difficulty. A typical garbled summary of these
early reports was that which appeared in the New York
Evening Post at the time of Dickens's death: "Ultimately
Charles Dickens went to the new country house [Gad's
Hill], accompanied by one of his daughters, and for her
sake invited his sister-in-law and a meritorious young
actress, to become inmates of their dwelling. It was not
long before this arrangement became a subject of serious
uneasiness to Mrs. Dickens. The 'green-eyed monster' is
said to have possessed her, and there arose those serious
misunderstandings which led to a dissolution of the marriage compact." [44] There seems little doubt that it was this

"meritorious young actress," then aged 19, and not Georgina, aged 32, whom Dickens was defending in the words, "as innocent as my young daughters."

This much, then, is evidence that no one has denied: Ellen Ternan acted with Dickens in the Manchester performances of *The Frozen Deep*, and her name was linked with his in the rumors that surrounded his separation. The final link is that hers was the first name mentioned in Dickens's will, and that he left her £1,000. Out of a total fortune of almost £100,000 it must be admitted that it was not an overgenerous bequest to a mistress of twelve years, if she was a mistress. But it was more than Mrs. Dickens received outright (she was to receive the income from £8,000 until death), and it was certainly overmuch for a casual acquaintance. No other friend, casual or intimate, received any mention at all except John Forster, Dickens's lifelong friend and later biographer, who received a gold watch and most of Dickens's manuscripts. The will itself stands as a final unnecessary act of injustice to Mrs. Dickens in its reiteration of her failure as a wife and mother. As John Bigelow remarked, "There may be a great diversity of opinion as to which of Mr. Dickens's works was the best, but the English speaking race, I imagine, will generally agree that his 'Will' was the worst." [45]

3

A Half Century of Rumor

SINCE Dickens's death much more has come to light, most of which, because it has not come from Dickens himself, has been unacceptable to the Dickensians, to whom the testimony of everyone else is suspect. It is presented here as part of the record; judgment of its validity or invalidity is left to the reader.

One of the earliest published statements about Dickens and "a lady not his wife," presumably Ellen Ternan, was made by Mrs. Julia Clara Byrne, wife of the proprietor of the *Morning Post,* in her autobiographical volume, *Gossip of the Century,* appearing in 1892. "Charles Dickens," she wrote, "was once by chance my fellow-traveller on the Boulogne packet; traveling with him was a lady not his wife, nor his sister-in-law, yet he strutted about the deck with the air of a man bristling with self-importance, every line of his face and every gesture of his limbs seemed haughtily to say—'Look at me; make the most of your chance. I am the great, the *only* Charles Dickens; whatever I may choose to do is justified by that fact.' . . . As a rule, the private life of a public man ought perhaps to be protected from the curiosity of the world; but when, having made himself a public man, he has had the bad taste to parade the unwarrantable acts of his private life so as to give public scandal, his conduct cannot escape criticism, and with it, the censure he has earned. . . .

None who know the history of [Mrs. Dickens's] outraged life, can respect Dickens as a man, however much they may admire him as a writer." [1]

Then, in 1910, the first volume of John Bigelow's five-volume *Retrospections of an Active Life* appeared. Bigelow was an American newspaperman, who served as United States minister to France during the Civil War. At the time of Dickens's death, newspapers mentioned him as one of the novelist's closest American friends, and the number of references to Dickens in Bigelow's diary indicate that he was certainly more than an acquaintance. In a passage in her unpublished diary, Mrs. James T. Fields, wife of the American publisher who helped arrange for Dickens's reading tour in 1867, wrote that Dickens "appears to have the deepest sympathy for men who are unfitly married and has really taken an especial fancy I think to John Bigelow . . . because his wife is such an incubus." [2] Bigelow, who was still living at the time the first volume appeared, allowed the following entry in his diary to stand, with no indication that he ever had reason to disbelieve it. Under date of March 10, 1860, he tells of meeting Mrs. Dickens at a dinner party at Thackeray's, and then goes on to record: "Mrs. Caulfield told me that a Miss Teman [*sic*]—I think that is the name—was the source of the difficulty between Mrs. Dickens and her husband. She played in private theatricals with Dickens, and he sent her a portrait in a brooch, which met with an accident requiring it to be sent to the jeweller's to be mended. The jeweller, noticing Mr. D's initials, sent it to his house. Mrs. Dickens's sister, who had always been in love with him and was jealous of Miss Teman, told Mrs. Dickens of the brooch, and she mounted her husband with comb

and brush. This, no doubt, was Mrs. Dickens's version
in the main." A few evenings later Bigelow saw "Miss
Teman" on the Haymarket stage and recorded: "She
seemed rather a small cause for such a serious result—
passably pretty and not much of an actress." [3]

Still another book of reminiscences, *Keeping Off
the Shelf*, by the English actress Blanche Galton (Mrs.
Thomas Whiffen), published in 1928, gives much the
same version of the Ternan story as Bigelow's, except that
for some reason Nelly is called Dickens's god-daughter.
In commenting upon the separation, she writes: "Tom
often told me that Dickens's god-daughter was one of the
causes of jealousy. The young lady was with the novelist
a great deal, and was in his company in the railway accident when the coach in which they sat hung down, sus-
pended by its coupling over a bridge. He never recovered
from the nervous shock that he then sustained." [4] Mrs.
Whiffen then repeats the story of the mixup at the jew-
eler's, though in her version the cause of the trouble was
a bracelet, not a brooch.

Mrs. Whiffen's account was dismissed by the Dickensians as the unreliable gossip of a garrulous old lady—
especially the suggestion, which she was the first to make,
that Nelly was with Dickens at the time he narrowly
escaped death in the Staplehurst railway accident of 1865.
In the Nonesuch edition of Dickens's letters, however,
appear two missives that would seem to corroborate the
garrulous old lady's statement and perhaps redeem the rest
of her account from charges of inaccuracy. On June 24,
1865, a few days after the railway accident which had
actually so shaken Dickens that was never to recover
fully from its effects, Dickens wrote a note to his serving-

man, John Thompson: "Take Miss Ellen tomorrow morning, a little basket of fresh fruit, a jar of clotted cream
from Tuckers, and a chicken, a pair of pigeons, or some
nice little bird. Also on Wednesday morning, and on Fri-
day morning, take her some other things of the same sort
—making a little variety each day." About the same time,
Dickens also wrote the head station master about a gold
watch, chain, charm, and other trinkets which had been
lost by a lady who had ridden in the same carriage with
him the day of the accident, adding, "I promised the lady
to make her loss known at headquarters." [5]

Other contemporary accounts have appeared from
time to time. Andrew de Ternant, writing to *Notes and
Queries* in 1933, quoted the comments Francesco Berger
had made to him about the Ternans. Berger, musical com-
poser and director of *The Frozen Deep* in 1858 and a
close friend of Dickens, stated that "he knew the Ternan
family very well, and often during the 'sixties played
games of cards at their house with the mother, daughter,
and Dickens, on Sunday evenings. This was generally
followed after supper by Ellen and Dickens singing duets
to his pianoforte accompaniment." [6] William Michael
Rossetti in his *Reminiscences* recalled a discussion of the
trouble between Dickens and his wife at the home of
Robert Stephen Rintoul, founder and editor of the *Spec-
tator*; "The verdict went dead against him," recorded
Rossetti.[7] Another account has appeared in the recently
published journal of Benjamin Moran. Under date of
June 12, 1858, appears the entry: "Hurlbut [Hurlbert],
who was in a few minutes since, tells me that Dickens
has separated from his wife after 25 years of married life,
and that C. Dickens, Jr. is to take charge of his mother's

house—while the daughters are to live with their father. Dickens sent for Thackeray some days ago rather angrily & accused him of circulating a slander; but Thackeray disabused him, & then Dickens told him what had been done. Rumor says this great novelist of the domestic hearth ran away with an actress; & his separation from his wife, altho it does not prove this story, does show that he really was not happy at home, altho' he wrote so well about that kind of thing." [8] In the recently published correspondence of Robert Browning with Isa Blagden, from the Browning Collection at the University of Texas, there is a reference to Ellen Ternan and her sister, Frances Eleanor Trollope. According to Professor Edward C. McAleer, editor of the correspondence, a letter from Isa Blagden to Browning had asked why he supposed Dickens had paid Mrs. Trollope so well for her novels (*Aunt Margaret's Trouble* and *Mabel's Progress*) which had run in his magazine, *All the Year Round*. "Her explanation," notes Professor McAleer, "was that Mrs. Trollope was the sister of Ellen Ternan, Dickens's mistress." Browning answered in a letter dated October 19, 1870: "As to the lady of your postscript—all I want to say is a little word about myself. You propounded as a knotty problem to me some time since 'How it came to pass that D. paid such sums for such novels as Mrs. T's': whereto I could but answer 'That I had no notion—but supposed there must be some reason beside the worth of the composition, if it were as poor as you assured me.' Now, for the sake of my character, pray ⟨let me⟩ tell you that the relationship between Mrs. T. and 'Miss T.' never crossed my mind: I must have heard it—very likely from yourself—but it took no hold of me: had it done so,—I should have been 'green' indeed, to give no better a guess at the solution of the riddle." [9]

These are the fullest statements left by contemporaries of Dickens, though other reports or hints of what could be disclosed if the writer were so disposed found their way into print from time to time.

Veiled references have appeared in ephemeral periodical accounts, such as: "It has been alleged against Dickens that he was guilty, not only of levity and unpardonable folly, but of absolute crimes—offenses heinous in their character and in contravention of both human and divine laws";[10] or, "He was guilty of an irreparable wrong, we say only what all men know, but which for reasons, sufficient and insufficient, most men keep to themselves. The great novelist had an instructive as well as an educated hatred of shams; and yet—we say it without bitterness—his whole life was, in a certain sense, a sham." [11] Even in Australia, where Dickens's emigrant sons may have done some talking, a dramatist named John Garraway wrote a play about Dickens's falling in love with a pretty actress named Miss Ternan during the rehearsals of *The Frozen Deep* at Manchester.[12]

A number of persons, some very close friends of Dickens, admitted quite openly that there were undivulged secrets about Dickens's private life which they were not at liberty to discuss. Donald Grant Mitchell hinted at the general conspiracy of silence when, in August, 1870, he wrote in an obituary article in *Hours at Home*, "Of the particulars of the matrimonial troubles of Mr. Dickens, though known to a great many, it is fitting that silence should be kept still." George Augustus Sala, a protégé of Dickens and one of his most devoted admirers, wrote angrily to the press in 1893 in protest against a projected

biography of the novelist, "There are circumstances connected with the later years of the illustrious novelist which
should not and must not be revealed for fifty years at the
very least." [13] Two years later he stated in his autobiography: "I say now, as I said after Dickens's death, the secret
was no affair of mine, and that so long as I lived it would
never be revealed by me. I should say that beyond the
members of Dickens's own family there are, now that
Wilkie Collins and Edmund Yates are gone, scarcely any
custodians of the secret besides myself." [14] Yates himself
had written: "It is not for me to apportion blame or to
mete out criticism. My intimacy with Dickens, his kindness to me, my devotion to him, were such that my lips
are sealed and my pen is paralysed as regards circumstances
which, if I felt less responsibility and less delicacy, I might
be at liberty to state." [15]

In 1899, Mrs. Lynn Linton, discussing Dickens and
Thackeray in her volume, *My Literary Life*, wrote: "Both
men could, and did, love deeply, passionately, madly, and
the secret history of their lives has yet to be written. It
never will be written now, and it is best that it should not
be. . . . Their close friends were also mine, and I heard
more than I saw. Many secret confidences were passed on
to me, which, of course, I have kept sacred; and both men
would have been surprised had they known how much
I knew of things uncatalogued and unpublished." [16] Much
is disclosed also in Mrs. Linton's description of Dickens
during the latter years of his life, when "no one could
move him; and his nearest and dearest friends were as
unwilling to face as they were unable to deflect the passionate pride which suffered neither counsel nor rebuke.
. . . He had a strain of hardness in his nature which

was like a rod of iron in his soul. . . . Nervous and arbi-
trary, he was of the kind to whom whims are laws, and
self control in contrary circumstances was simply an im-
possibility." One of those "nearest and dearest friends"
corroborates Mrs. Linton's description of Dickens's personality. Though an idolizer and intimate of Dickens over
a number of years, Edmund Yates wrote of him: "He was
imperious in the sense that his life was conducted on the
sic volo sic jubeo principle, and that everything gave way
before him. The society in which he mixed, the hours
which he kept, the opinions which he held, his likes and
dislikes, his ideas of what should or should not be, were
all settled by himself, not merely for himself, but for all
those brought into connection with him, and it was never
imagined they could be called in question." [17]

Lyndon Orr, writing on Dickens for the New York
Bookman in 1912, said of the separation scandal: "This
whole episode remains a lasting blot upon the memory
of Dickens. Of his manner of life thereafter it is unnecessary to speak. He lived like other Englishmen of his class,
and he and his friend Bulwer-Lytton became standing
examples of the sort of domestic infelicity which is con-
tinually on view and which invites the stares and unseemly
jocularity of the rabble. In the case of Lytton, however,
it was Lady Lytton who was blameable for this publicity.
In the case of Dickens it was the man, and not the woman,
who deserved the blame. It is, indeed, greatly to the honour
of Mrs. Dickens that she preserved unbroken the silence
and the dignity which her distinguished husband so ut-
terly forgot." [18]

Finally, perhaps the most influential statement of
belief in the Ternan story was that expressed by the uni-

versally respected and beloved "Father of the House of
Commons," T. P. O'Connor—"Tay Pay,"—who was an
intimate friend of the Dickens family, especially of Kate
Dickens Perugini, over a number of years. In his "Table
Talk" column in *T. P.'s Weekly* for September 29, 1928,
the Irish journalist wrote a spirited defense of Dickens
against the picture of him presented in C. E. Bechhofer
Roberts's fictionized biography, *This Side Idolatry*. O'Connor then went on to remark casually: "Of course, Dickens
sinned, and very few men of genius have not sinned in
the same way. Unhappy at home, he sought relief abroad.
The story of Ellen Terman [*sic*] may one day be told; but
who to-day would form a scathing and foul indictment
of any of our contemporary writers because there entered
into their unhappy inner lives some other woman who
gave them compensation and comfort? There is nothing
very remarkable in the story, and it should be judged with
that indulgence with which temperamental defects that
usually accompany literary genius are considered." Dickens would have sympathized with O'Connor's point of
view, having himself remarked concerning a similar charge
against an unnamed "venerable old gentleman," "Good
God if such sins were to be visited upon all of us and to
hunt us down through life, what man would escape!" [19]

There is also the mute evidence of the silences, which
sometimes tell more than words. If Ellen was just a "meritorious young actress" who remained a friend of Dickens's
daughters and was sufficiently close to the Dickens family
to be left £1,000 in his will, why is there practically no
mention of her in his letters, or at least in the letters which
have been allowed to survive? Shortly after the separation
Dickens suddenly decided to make a huge bonfire of all

the letters that had ever been written him, a ceremony repeated at intervals until his death.[20] Knowing well that every letter of the "Inimitable Boz" would be preserved by the addressee, Dickens would undoubtedly have taken care to guard his secret well; if there were letters to Ellen (and we shall see that there were), he would have urged her to follow his own practice of burning all correspondence.[21]

Georgina Hogarth and Dickens's elder daughter Mamie, as editors of the first edition of Dickens's letters, adopted a policy of presenting Dickens as all sweetness and light. As is made evident by comparing the original manuscripts with the printed versions, they kept his less admirable traits out of sight by suppressing or toning down many passages relating to such things as his conviviality, his passion for money, his attraction to a number of young women at various times, and of course all mention, however innocent, of the Ternan family. Even Dickens's normal endearing phrases to and about his wife until just before the separation were omitted from the family edition of letters, presumably to support the legend that he never really loved her.[22] Numerous passages in the letters from Dickens to Georgina, now in the Huntington Library, have been cut out with scissors. Large gaps in the correspondence indicate that many letters must have been entirely destroyed. Georgina herself in an unpublished letter to Frederick Ouvry dated May 5, 1879,[23] speaks of having destroyed letters of a kind too personal for publication.

Most of the many letters from Dickens to John Forster seem also to have disappeared; we have only those portions of them that Forster chose to incorporate in the

Life.[24] The biography itself passes over the separation with the briefest comment. There is hardly a mention of Mrs. Dickens in all three volumes, and no reference at all to the "meritorious young actress" who supposedly came to Gad's Hill to console Dickens's daughters after the forced withdrawal of their mother. Forster struggled a long time with that fateful third volume, writing to Longfellow in the midst of it, "Whether or not I shall live to finish the sorrowful task—more painful and heavy to me than I could ever hope to convey to you—I do not know. 'Shadows, clouds, and darkness rest upon it.' " [25]

For sixty years the "shadows, clouds, and darkness" prevailed, as biographer after biographer was content to do no more than reshuffle the same old pieces. Then, in 1934, the Dickens legend received a blow which sent it reeling. Thomas Wright began publishing the first new material on Dickens since Forster's biography, material he had been collecting for over thirty years. On April 3 of that year he published in the London *Daily Express* an article on Dickens and Ellen Ternan entitled, "Charles Dickens Began his Honeymoon," which was followed the next year by his biography of the novelist. According to Wright, Ellen had been Dickens's mistress from "shortly after the separation" until Dickens's death. He got the account at first hand from Canon William Benham, an Anglican clergyman to whom the conscience-ridden Ellen had told the whole story. Benham was Vicar of Margate, where Ellen's husband, George Wharton Robinson, conducted a school. The Canon was a close friend of the Robinsons for a number of years and told Wright that Ellen had given him the pen with which Dickens wrote *Edwin Drood.*[26]

Wright gives for the first time an extended circumstantial account of Dickens's infatuation for the young actress, the quarrel with Mrs. Dickens over the bracelet, Dickens's frenzied behavior toward his wife and her family, his forcing them to sign the recantation, and his setting up of a second "establishment" for Ellen. Throughout the account, Wright hints at Ellen's unhappiness during the May-December relationship; critics since Wright, sensing its tragic undertones for both Dickens and Ellen, have drawn attention to possible echoes in the portrayals of Estella Provis in *Great Expectations*, Bella Wilfer in *Our Mutual Friend*, and Helena Landless in *Edwin Drood*.

Although some reviewers hailed Wright's revelations as the most important contribution to the biography of Dickens since Forster, the Dickens cultists were goaded to almost hysterical vilification, charging that his whole case was based upon completely unreliable hearsay evidence. Wright's postponement of the publication of his findings until after the death of all the principals was not interpreted as the behavior of a gentleman who wished to spare embarrassment to these protagonists, but as that of a charlatan who waited until all were dead who could deny his statements.[27] Yet Wright was a scholar of considerable reputation, the author of fourteen biographies, editor of the letters of Cowper and other literary figures, compiler of early ballads, and founder of the Cowper Society, the John Payne Society, and the Blake Society. Furthermore, Wright himself had been an ardent Dickensian and had worked arduously for the establishment of a Dickens museum in London. The charges all but broke him. He set about to add more facts to his account

and searched out the records of the "establishments" where
Nelly lived at various times. He talked to people who remembered her and who remembered a man namd Charles
who lived with her. But editors were reluctant about
publishing his findings. He died the next year, in 1936,
and these findings were at last made public in his posthumous autobiography, *Thomas Wright of Olney.* The per-
secution continues. As recently as 1951 a writer has said
of Wright that he "abandoned common standards of decency and the canons of genuine biography to pander to
the desires of those who relish sensationalism." [28]

A second blow fell in 1939. In February of that year
a woman, manuscript in hand, appeared in the London
office of the late Walter Dexter, editor of *The Dickensian.*
The woman was Miss Gladys Storey and the manuscript
was that of the book published later that year under the
title, *Dickens and Daughter.* Mr. Dexter, respected leader
of the Dickensians for a generation, whose labors included
the monumental task of editing the Nonesuch edition of
letters, had refused to accept Wright's account. But the
manuscript placed before him on that February day in
1939 convinced him of the validity of the Ternan story.
Asked for his advice about publishing the manuscript, he
could only say to Miss Storey, "The Truth at last!" [29] And
it is significant that *The Dickensian,* so long as it continued under his editorship—until his death in 1944—
contained no more denials of Dickens's liaison with Ellen
Ternan.

Miss Storey's dramatic volume should assuredly have
convinced the most skeptical. It came as a voice from the
grave, the voice of Kate Dickens Perugini, second daughter of Dickens. It was an important contribution to Dick-

ens biography because it not only presented the facts
which Wright had, in one biographer's words, only "sniffed
out," but also underscored the common decency of presenting those facts as an act of long-overdue justice to the
memory of a maligned woman—Mrs. Dickens. It is strange
that those who have most to say about protecting the name
and reputation of Dickens rise to no such defense of his
wife, subscribing nonchalantly to the notion that she was
all the things Dickens said she was at the time of the
separation—lazy, stupid (if not unbalanced), selfish, an
unfit mother for her ten children, whom she never loved
and who never loved her. Innumerable comments tucked
away in contemporary letters and memoirs, some still unpublished, which no Dickensian has bothered to assemble,
give quite another picture. Miss Storey, an intimate friend
of Kate Perugini over a period of many years, wrote her
book, to quote her own words, "in fidelity to my pledged
word to Mrs. Kate Perugini," [30] and she claimed that her
account was based on the journal in which she had recorded the day-to-day reminiscences of Dickens's daughter.
Giving Mrs. Dickens's side of the separation story for the
first time, *Dickens and Daughter* carries the dedication,
"In loving memory of my friend, Mrs. Kate Perugini,
and to the memory of her mother, Mrs. Charles Dickens";
and a passage from St. Matthew stands as the epigraph:
"For there is nothing covered, that shall not be revealed;
and hid, that shall not be known."

Dickens and Daughter is obviously the work of a
nonprofessional writer who was interested only in fulfill-
ing the promise made to Kate to write down the story as
she heard it from her lips. Miss Storey reveals that at one
time Kate, conscience-stricken by the way in which Dick-

ens and all the children (through fear of their father) had treated Mrs. Dickens, wrote out a life of her father which was to be deposited in the British Museum. Later she burned the manuscript. "I told only half the truth about my father," she said, "and a half-truth is worse than a lie, for this reason I destroyed what I had written. But the truth *must be told* when the time comes—after my death." [31]

The truth, even as stated in the direct and artless language used by Miss Storey, demolished Dickens's plaster pedestal. "My father was like a madman when my mother left home," Kate told Miss Storey. "This affair brought out all that was worst—all that was weakest in him. He did not care a damn what happened to any of us. Nothing could surpass the misery and unhappiness of our home." [32] Then the whole story of her father's infatuation for the young actress and the tragic consequences for all concerned is unfolded—this time not through the by-channels of gossip and rumor, but by one of the victims of the tragedy. Mrs. Perugini, who described Nelly as "the small fair-haired rather pretty actress," told Miss Storey that she "came like a breath of spring into the hard-working life of Charles Dickens—and enslaved him. She flattered him—he was ever appreciative of praise—and though 'she was not a good actress she had brains, which she used to educate herself, to bring her mind more on a level with his own. Who could blame her? . . . He had the world at his feet. She was a young girl of eighteen, elated and proud to be noticed by him.' " [33] As for Dickens —he found the flush of youth rekindled within him, and "pursued the realization of it with the same energy and thoroughness he applied to everything he set his heart on doing."

Mrs. Perugini's chief concern in these later years when she was retelling the story to her friend was for her mother. "My poor mother," she said, "was afraid of my father. She was never allowed to express an opinion—never allowed to say what she felt." And then she added, "Ah! We were *all* very wicked not to take her part." [34] She was recalling, with intense remorse, how the children had neglected their mother; she and her sister Mamie (to the end of her life completely dominated by her father) had even at one time taken music lessons directly across the street from where Mrs. Dickens was then living, but had never stopped to see her. Kate Dickens summed up the whole drama in the words, "More tragic and far-reaching in its effects was the association of Charles Dickens and Ellen Ternan and their resultant son (who died in infancy),[35] than that of Nelson and Lady Hamilton and their daughter." [36]

Though staggered by Miss Storey's book, the defenders of the Dickens legend were not ready to accept its revelations. Again they charged that the volume was a tissue of gossip and hearsay, unsupported by real "evidence." Unable to deny that Miss Storey had long been an intimate friend of Kate Perugini, they resorted to implications that the latter was of unbalanced mind in her later years. Few of them appear to have taken note of a letter written by George Bernard Shaw to the London *Times* answering such charges. "Your reviewer of *Dickens and Daughter,*" he wrote, "bases a strong disapproval of its publication to some extent on a conjecture that Mrs.

Perugini's mind, giving way at the end of her long life, upset her judgment as to her mother's wishes." Shaw then stated emphatically: "I had a serious conversation with Mrs. Perugini on the subject about forty years ago. My last conversation with her took place shortly before her death. Her mind was not in the least enfeebled. It was in the same condition as at the end of the last century." As to hints against the integrity and motives of Miss Storey, Shaw went on to say: "I have no doubt that Miss Storey has carried out the wishes, early and late, of Mrs. Perugini in publishing her book. And I have the best reason for believing that Mrs. Perugini first took up the matter at her mother's request." [37] Then Shaw, a lifelong and ardent Dickensian himself, ended his letter with the dry comment: "The facts of the case may be in bad taste. Facts often are."

Since 1939 most critics and biographers, with the exception of those few who still feel that legend is more important than fact, have accepted the Ternan story and have been reinterpreting the later novels in the light of that story. The appearance of the Nonesuch edition of Dickens's letters in 1938 made available for the first time many unpublished letters and portions of others that had been suppressed by Georgina Hogarth, John Forster, and minor compilers. It is true that no direct mention of Ellen Ternan's close relation to Dickens was made in all three volumes (containing almost 9,000 letters)—an omission which caused the zealous Dickensian, J. W. T. Ley, to greet the publication with the words, "At every turn the ghouls are thwarted." [38] What Mr. Ley did not know was that in the course of years great numbers of Dickens letters had found their way into American libraries, and that

Mr. Dexter was not able to examine these letters person-
ally; many letters were unavoidably omitted and others
were reprinted in their earlier garbled or expurgated
form.[39] The handsomely printed Nonesuch volumes certainly added a great deal to public knowledge of Dickens
and his times, but they are far from definitive. A new
edition is in progress, under the general editorship of Mr.
Humphry House of Oxford University; until that complete edition appears, scholars must compare the Nonesuch letters with the originals, word by word and paragraph by paragraph, if they wish to get the facts. In
addition, as has been pointed out, many letters were destroyed by members of the family, an action which was
their privilege but which renders any generalizations about
what is not found in the total collection open to some
question.

A good example of the revelations to be discovered
in long-suppressed letters is the correspondence of Dickens
with Miss Burdett Coutts, recently published in the London *Times* by Mr. K. J. Fielding.[40] Dickens was particularly proud of his long-standing friendship with Miss
Coutts, one of the wealthiest philanthropists in England,
and he is here revealed at his most desperate as he tries
to explain his separation. Miss Coutts apparently was determined to get at the real cause, and her blunt question-
ing drove Dickens to the wildest self-justification in the
following letter, the original manuscript of which is now
in the possession of the New York Public Library:

. . . My dear friend, I quite understand and appreciate your
feeling that there must be no reservation between us, and that
we must not have a skeleton in a closet, and make belief [*sic*] it
is not there. But I must not enter on the wretched subject, upon

false pretences. I must not do what would make my dear girls out to be a sort of phenomena, and what would make my own relations with Mrs. Dickens, incomprehensible. Since we spoke of her before, she has caused me unspeakable agony of mind; and I must plainly put before you what I know to be true, and what nothing shall induce me to affect to doubt. She does not—and she never did—care for the children; and the children do not—and never did—care for her. The little play that is acted in your Drawing-room[41] is not the truth, and the less the children play it, the better for themselves, because they know it is not the truth. (If I stood before you at this moment and told you what difficulty we have to get Frank, for instance, to go near his mother, or keep near his mother, you would stand amazed.) As for Mrs. Dickens's "simplicity" in speaking of me and my doings, O my dear Miss Coutts do I not know that the weak hand that never could help or serve my name in the least, has struck at it—in conjunction with the wickedest people, whom I have loaded with benefits! I want to communicate with her no more. I want to forgive her and forget her.

I could not begin a course of references to her, without recording, as between you and me, what I know to be true. It would be monstrous to myself, and to the children also. From Walter away in India, to little Plornish at Gad's Hill there is a grim knowledge among them, as familiar to them as their knowledge of Daylight, that what I now write, is the plain bare fact. She has always disconcerted them; they have always disconcerted her; and she is glad to be rid of them, and they are glad to be rid of her.

It would be wise to recall here that according to Miss Storey Dickens himself once remarked to his daughter, "We should always remember . . . that letters are but ephemeral: we must not be affected too much either by those which praise us or by others written in the heat of the moment." [42]

Little further comment need be made except that the

correspondence between Miss Coutts and Dickens, which had been extensive for a number of years, soon dropped to a few formal exchanges of condolences or holiday greetings. In the voluminous collection of Dickens-Coutts letters recently acquired by the Pierpont Morgan Library, only a very few of which were published in Charles C. Osborne's edition of that correspondence in 1931, there is no letter from Dickens between December, 1858, and January, 1860. On January 30, Dickens wrote to thank Miss Coutts for assisting Charley in his application for a position with Barings House. On March 13, 1860, in a letter on the same subject, Dickens wrote: "I cannot trust myself on the ground that lies trembling at the point of my pen. Many reasons, old and new, unnerve me." On August 3, 1860, Dickens wrote an acknowledgment of a letter of sympathy at the time of his brother's death, following which there is no other letter until February 12, 1864, when Dickens acknowledged a second letter of sympathy at the time of his son Walter's tragic death. In his response Dickens wrote: "Do not think me unimpressed by certain words in your letter concerning forgiveness and tenderness when I say that I do not claim to have anything to forgive—that if I had, I hope and believe I would forgive freely—but that a page in my life which once had writing on it, has become absolutely blank, and that it is not in my power to pretend that it has a solitary word upon it." It is interesting in this connection that Sir William Hardman, a close friend of Mrs. Dickens, wrote of her grief over the death of this son Walter that it was "much enhanced by the fact that her husband has not taken any notice of the event to her, either by letter or otherwise. If anything were wanting to sink

Charles Dickens to the lowest depths of my esteem, *this* fills up the measure of his iniquity. As a writer, I admire him; as a man, I despise him." [43] It would appear from Dickens's words to Miss Coutts that she, like Sir William, had thought his behavior to his wife deserving of reproach. There are only three more letters in the Dickens-Coutts collection at the Morgan Library, one thanking Miss Coutts for her Christmas greeting, one thanking her for her expression of concern after the Staplehurst accident in 1865, and a final one, dated February 6, 1866, written in behalf of a clergyman acquaintance of Dickens.

After the separation, Miss Coutts went out of her way to be kind to Mrs. Dickens, of whose existence she had been hardly aware beforehand. She even offered Mrs. Dickens a refuge in her home when the separation took place; and at the time of Dickens's death, when his wife was not allowed to see him or invited to attend his funeral, Miss Coutts went to console Mrs. Dickens at her home, not Georgina Hogarth at Gad's Hill. She was an intelligent woman and a woman of unquestioned integrity, who appears to have made her own decision about the course of action taken by Dickens at the time of the separation.

Certain passages in the Nonesuch edition take on new meaning in the light of Wright's and Miss Storey's revelations. We have already mentioned the note about Ellen in connection with the Staplehurst accident. Remarks such as the following, written to Macready just before the separation, carry one directly into the troubled mind and heart of Dickens: "I am devising all sorts of things in my mind, and am in a state of energetic restlessness. . . . What a dream it is, this work and strife, and how little we do in the dream after all! Only last night, in my sleep, I was bent upon getting over a perspective of barriers, with my hands and feet bound. Pretty much what we are all about, waking, I think?"[44] And again, in a letter to Wilkie Collins: "I want to escape from myself. For, when I *do* start up and stare myself seedily in the face, as happens to be my case at present, my blankness is inconceivable—indescribable—my misery, amazing. . . . The domestic unhappiness remains so strong upon me that I can't write, and (waking) can't rest, one minute. I have never known a moment's peace or content, since the last night of The Frozen Deep. I do suppose that there never was a man so seized and rended by one spirit."[45] About the same time, in answer to Forster's objections to the proposed reading tours, Dickens wrote, "I must do *something,* or I shall wear my heart away. I can see no better thing to do that is half so hopeful in itself, or half so well suited to my restless state."[46] Later, immediately after the separation had been made public, Dickens complained to his friend Edmund Yates: "If you could know how much I have felt within this last month, and what a sense of wrong has been upon me, and what a strain and struggle I have lived under, you would see that my heart is so jagged and rent and out of shape, that it does not this day leave me hand enough to shape these words."[47]

Of particular interest also are the many letters Dickens wrote to friends at the time of the separation, often in response to their expressions of sympathy, such as that to the Rev. Edward Tagart, written on June 14, 1858: "Though I have unquestionably suffered deeply from being lied about with a wonderful recklessness, I am not so weak or wrong-headed as to be in the least changed by it.

I know the world to have just as much good in it as it had before; and no one has better reason to thank God for the friendship it contains, than I have. So I hope to regain my composure in a steady manner, and to live to be good and true to my innocent people who have been traduced along with me." [48] Of even greater interest to readers today is the letter to another friend, W. F. de Cerjat, in which Dickens wrote: "I know very well that a man who has won a very conspicuous position, has incurred in the winning of it, a heavy debt to the knaves and fools, which he must be content to pay, over and over again, all through his life. Further, I know equally well that I can never hope that anyone out of my house can ever comprehend my domestic story. I will not complain. I have been heavily wounded, but I have covered the wound up, and left it to heal. Some of my children or some of my friends will do me right if I ever need it in the time to come. And I hope that my books will speak for themselves and me, when I and my faults and virtues, my fortunes and misfortunes are all forgotten." [49]

Besides the foregoing and other similar letters in the Nonesuch volumes, there are many yet unpublished, written to various friends at the time of their separation, in which Dickens, or Georgina on Dickens's behalf, tried to explain his situation (Stephen Leacock once wrote that Dickens "lived and died explaining himself").[50] A number of these letters suggest that the recipient initiate a word-of-mouth campaign in Dickens's behalf, as in the following letter to Mrs. Gore, a popular woman novelist of the day who had a wide circle of influential friends. Because it is typical of all such letters written at the time, the greater part of it is here quoted in full:

...er, but that we quietly accept all that, and do not blame
...ay, and only seek to make the best of it.

...What I tell you, is quite at your disposal to tell again, when
...where you will.[51]

To Emile de la Rue, a more intimate friend than
... Gore, Dickens wrote in a more facetious spirit a few
...ths before the final break with Mrs. Dickens, giving
...e hint of the real reasons behind the separation:

...een ourselves (I beckon Madame De la Rue nearer with
...orefinger, and whisper this with a serio-comic smile), I don't
...on better in these later times with a certain poor lady you
...v of, than I did in the earlier Peschiere days. Much worse.
...h worse. Neither do the children, elder or younger. Neither
...she get on with herself, or be anything but unhappy. (She
...been excruciatingly jealous of, and has obtained positive
...fs of my being on the most confidential terms with, at least
...en Thousand Women of various conditions in life, every
...dition in life, since we left Genoa. Please to respect me for
...vast experience.) What we should do, or what the Girls
...ld be, without Georgy, I cannot imagine. She is the active
...t of the house, and the children dote upon her. Enough of
... We put the Skeleton away in the cupboard, and very few
...ple, comparatively, know of its existence.[52]

The total impression after reading through Dickens's
...espondence during the months before and after the
...aration is that Dickens was seized by a sense of panic
...t the discovery of the real skeleton in his cupboard
...uld destroy him. At the same time, however, this sense
...panic was strangely coupled with a strong sense of
...fidence that he could and would control the public
...had learned to know so well during the twenty years
...ad idolized him.

I have heard such thronging multi
inexplicable lies about myself during the
bewilders me to find you in possession of

—Except that you are not to suppo
to be "divided." Charley takes care of hi
request, and all the rest remain with r
keeping my house. Charley undertakes l
ment as an act of duty, and on the expre
is to be nothing in the nature of a partin

Believe me, I had already so strongly
long absences and so forth, that I had r
proposed it and stood out upon it. That l
I really believe to be in the nature of the
fault of Mrs. Dickens.

Our separation is the natural end of a
felt the force of our example, and have,
it and sacrificed to it. But it would be a po
mad myself, or to drive Mrs. Dickens ma
the two results must have happened, if v
together.

There is no anger or ill-will between
slightest. Our elder children are at least as
must be, as we are. Between them and m
dence as absolute and perfect as if we w
Dickens's sister (who has devoted her who
brought them up from their cradles), and
servant, always in Mrs. Dickens's confiden
with us for sixteen years, both know per
have long exerted themselves to prevent
that it has become inevitable.

I do not doubt that we shall all be m
I only want to impress upon you that it is c
done; that whatever doubt or passion the:
either side, has already died out; that I an
to forgive and forget, and live at peace; bu
day for both, when two such strongly cor

toge
the

and

Mr
mo
son

Bet
my
get
kno
Mu
can
has
pro
Fif
con
this
wo
spi
this
pec

co
se
th
wo
of
co
he
it

There is one other letter in the Nonesuch edition
which makes one of the most revealing statements Dickens
ever put in writing about Ellen Ternan and his feelings
for her. The letter is addressed to Mrs. Frances Elliot,
née Dickinson, an actress friend of Ellen's who had taken
a minor part in the fateful production of *The Frozen
Deep*. Apparently Mrs. Elliot had offered to defend "N"
[Nelly] in some way or other, and Dickens answers: "I
feel your affectionate letter truly and deeply, but it would
be inexpressibly painful to N to think that you knew her
history. She has no suspicion that your assertion of your
friend against the opposite powers, ever brought you to
the knowledge of it. She would not believe that you could
see her with my eyes, or know her with my mind. Such
a presentation is impossible. It would distress her for the
rest of her life. I thank you none the less, but it is quite
out of the question. If she could hear that, she could not
have the pride and self reliance which (mingled with the
gentlest nature) has borne her, alone, through so much." [53]

The pathos here, both for Dickens and for Ellen,
strikes as deep a chord as anything in all his novels.

4

Dickens Speaks

Now WE COME to some of the new evidence that the
Dickensians have been demanding. This time the evidence
is given by Dickens himself, in uncontestable statements
written down in the bright blue ink so familiar to the
Dickens scholar and collector. The first two pieces of this
evidence have been in print (one in full, one in summary), but have somehow been overlooked by all the biographers. The rest is published here for the first time.

The first is a letter, now part of the Huntington Library collection of manuscripts, which was first published
by Professor Franklin P. Rolfe in *Nineteenth-Century
Fiction*.[1] This letter was written a few months after the
separation to William Henry Wills, subeditor of *Household Words* under Dickens, and later co-partner as well
as subeditor of *All the Year Round*. It was not included
in R. C. Lehmann's edition of the Dickens-Wills correspondence, nor in the Nonesuch letters. Because of its
extreme interest, it is here reprinted in full:

> Tavistock House,
> Tavistock Square, London, W.C.
> Monday Night Twenty Fifth October 1858

My Dear Wills

Since I left you tonight, I have heard of a case of such
extraordinary, and (apparently) Dangerous and unwarrantable

48

conduct in a Policeman, that I shall take it as a great kindness if you will go to Yardley in Scotland Yard when you know the facts for yourself, and ask him to enquire what it means.

I am quite sure that if the circumstances as they stand were stated in the Times, there would be a most prodigious public uproar.

Before you wait upon Yardley, saying that you know the young ladies and can answer for them and for their being in all things most irreproachable in themselves and most respectably connected in all ways, and that you want to know what the Devil the mystery means—see the young ladies and get the particulars from them.

No. 31 Berners Street Oxford Street, is the address of the young ladies, and the young ladies are Miss Maria and Miss Ellen Ternan, both of whom you know. You are to understand, between you and me, that I have sent the eldest sister to Italy, to complete a musical education—that Mrs. Ternan is gone with her, to see her comfortably established at Florence; and that our two little friends are left together, in the meanwhile, in the family lodgings. Observe that they don't live about in furnished lodgings, but have their own furniture. They have not been many weeks in their present address, and I strongly advised Mrs. Ternan to move from their last one, which I thought unwholesome.

Can you call and see them between 3 and 5 tomorrow (Tuesday)? They will expect you, unless you write to the contrary. If you can't go, will you write and make another appointment.

(N.B. Maria is a good deal looked after. And my suspicion is, that the Policeman in question has been suborned to find out all about their domesticity by some "Swell." If so, there can be no doubt that the man ought to be dismissed.)

They will tell you his No. They don't seem so clear about his letter, but that is no matter. The division on duty in Berners Street, is of course ascertainable by Scotland Yard authorities.

Ever faithfully,

CD.

The letter needs little comment. It introduces evidence, not mentioned by either Wright or Miss Storey, that Dickens sent Frances Eleanor Ternan and her mother to Florence at his own expense and that the two younger girls were left in new lodgings, which it is strongly hinted Dickens himself arranged for, a very short while after his separation from his wife. Certainly the objections of the Dickensians to the "monstrous" statement that the mother of Ellen could have visited her and played cards with her seducer at the "establishment," as Francesco Berger stated, or allowed that establishment to be taken out in her name, as Wright stated,[2] seem to be answered here. As Professor Rolfe observed, Mrs. Ternan "apparently was not averse to having him support her daughters." Less than a year later the Ternans were living at another address, 2 Houghton Place, Ampthill Square, N.W., an address Dickens gives in a letter recommending Mrs. Ternan and Maria for parts in a current theatrical production.[3] In an unpublished letter now in the Huntington Library collection, dated July 1, 1859, Dickens asks Wills to "send round" to the printer for the revises of some of his current manuscript, and then goes on to request that he "post them to Miss Ellen Ternan, 2 Houghton Place, Ampthill Square, N.W."

The letter to Wills about the policeman is especially interesting in the light of Dickens's later relations with Ellen's eldest sister. It was probably on the trip to Florence mentioned here that Fanny Ternan and her mother first met the Trollopes, through the letter of introduction from Dickens already mentioned. In 1866, when Fanny went to Thomas Adolphus Trollope's as companion-governess to his motherless child, Dickens wrote to Trollope:

"Truly, as you say, it seems a long while ago that I gave
[Fanny] a letter of commendation to your kindness.
Though it is but a few years, she has experienced such
warmth of friendship from you and yours, that I shouldn't
wonder if it seemed to her a life. I am heartily glad, both
for her sake and for yours, that she is with you." [4] A few
months later Dickens wrote his congratulations on Trollope's marriage to Fanny—"No friend that you have can
be more truly attached to you than I am. I congratulate
you with all my heart. . . . I little thought what an important master of ceremonies I was when I first gave your
present wife an introduction to your mother." [5]

There is another interesting reference to Fanny
in an unpublished letter now in the Pierpont Morgan
Library. The letter, dated July 23, 1858, is addressed to
Richard Smith Spofford,[6] a cousin of the Ternans living
in America; its context implies that Spofford had written
the eldest of his cousins after having heard the gossip
about Dickens and an English actress named Ternan. If
so, he apparently expressed his disbelief in the gossip,
whereupon Dickens hurried off a letter of appreciation:

"Your cousin Fanny has shewn me a letter of yours
in which reference is made to me. I would not for the
world do her or you the wrong of giving you any assurance upon a subject on which your own generous nature
is perfectly clear. But what I wish to do is to thank you
most heartily for the comfort and strength I have derived
from the contemplation of your character as it is expressed
in that letter beyond the possibility of mistake, and to
convey to you, in a manner as plain and unaffected as
your own, my admiration of the noble instinct with which
the upright know the upright, all the broad world over.

Your cousin well deserves to be its subject. From the first month, I think, of my knowing your cousin Fanny, I have confided in her, have taken great interest in her, and have highly respected her. You may be sure (as I know her mother and sisters are, and as I know, my own two ·daughters are), that there could not live upon this earth a man more blamelessly and openly her friend than I am, or to whom her honor could be dearer than it is to me."

A second dramatic and significant Dickens manuscript has been neglected by critics and biographers, though attention was directed to it in 1943 by John D. Gordan, curator of the Berg Collection at the New York Public Library, in an article in *Bookmen's Holiday*.[7] This manuscript has a definite relation to the letters quoted above because it reveals that Nelly went to Florence to stay with her sister during the time that Dickens toured America in 1867–1868. Just before he left England, Dickens left several pages of memoranda for his subeditor W. H. Wills, giving instructions regarding business matters and financial arrangements for the Dickens family. One paragraph of these memoranda was heavily inked out on the manuscript, either by Wills himself or perhaps by Georgina when she borrowed the Wills correspondence for use in her edition of the letters. In the R. C. Lehmann edition of the correspondence the memoranda are given, but this paragraph is omitted. Dr. Gordan, through the aid of infrared photography, was able to read the obliterated portion, and reported his findings in the article which he called "The Secret of Dickens's Memoranda." He did not, however, reproduce the original manuscript in its exact wording, so it is published here for the first time:

NELLY

If she needs any help will come to you, or if she changes her address, you will immediately let me know if she changes. Until then it will be Villa Trollope, a Ricorboli, Firenze, Italy [Here it is again more plainly written:

VILLA TROLLOPE

a RICORBOLI

FIRENZE

ITALY][8]

On the day after my arrival out I will send you a short Telegram at the office. Please copy its exact words, (as they will have a special meaning for her), and post them to her as above by the very next post after receiving my telegram. And also let Gad's Hill know—and let Forster know—what the telegram is.

A later note in the memoranda, not inked out but suppressed by Lehmann, states that Forster "knows Nelly as you do, and will do anything for her if you want anything done."

Villa Trollope was, of course, the residence of Tom Trollope. In his autobiography, Trollope mentions that his sister-in-law (unnamed, but probably Ellen since he usually refers to his other sister-in-law, Maria, by her married name) was staying with them when they visited the Vesuvius eruption in January, 1868.[9] He also mentions that she again came to them from England in September, 1870, a few months after Dickens's death.[10] According to a letter from Browning to Isa Blagden, Tom and Fanny had been in London toward the end of 1867, and so Ellen may well have returned with them to Florence.[11]

Lehmann had printed the text of Dickens's telegram to Wills upon his arrival in America—"Safe and well expect good letter full of hope," [12]—which, as Dr. Gordan observes, was innocuous enough, though according to Dickens it had a "special meaning" for Nelly. "What the message meant to Nelly," Gordan continues, "will probably never be known."

Ironically, while I was going through the Dickens manuscripts at the New York Public Library some years ago, I ran across the answer to the puzzle of that "special meaning." I was leafing through the pages of a very small pocket diary for the year 1867, containing only the most inconsequential single-line daily entries, when I suddenly discovered, hidden away in some blank pages in the back, what would seem to be the code for that message to Nelly. It reads:

> Tel: all well means
> > *you come*
> Tel: safe and well, means
> > *you don't come*
> To Wills. Who sends the Te. on to
> > Villa Trollope
> > > fuori la porta S'Niccolo
> > > Florence

Dickens had hoped to bring Nelly to America!

No doubt there were many to advise against such an action, and Dickens reluctantly sent off the cable beginning, "Safe and well." As early as 1859, in a suppressed passage of a letter to his manager Arthur Smith, Dickens stated that he had refused the offer of a reading tour in America "for a private reason, rendering a long voyage and absence particularly painful to me." [13] Again, in 1866, he wrote his later manager, George Dolby, "I have had a

very large proposal from America, but cannot bear the
thought of the distance and absence." [14] And here, even
after his departure for America, Dickens was still rebelling
against the separation from Nelly. It is clear that love for
the young actress twenty-eight years his junior was as
sincere and deep-seated as it was passionate.

There are many other passages in the letters Dickens
wrote home to Wills from his American tour which reveal
how much he regretted the separation from Ellen. These
letters are now in the Huntington Library, and the passages
referring to Ellen have been obliterated with the same pen
that inked out the memorandum. Most of these occur at
the beginnings of the letters and indicate that Dickens was
enclosing letters to Nelly, to be forwarded by Wills. Again,
transcriptions[15] made with the aid of infrared photography
are published here for the first time:

(November 21, 1867) Will you specially observe, my dear fellow
what I am going to add. After this present mail, I shall address
Nelly's letters to your care, for I do not quite know where she
will be. But she will write to you, and instruct you where to
forward them. In any interval between your receipt of one or
more, and my Dear Girl's so writing to you, keep them by you.

(December 3) *The enclosed letter to your care as usual.*

(December 6) Enclosed is another letter for my dear girl.

(December 10) Enclosed is another letter for my dear girl, to
your usual care and exactness. By this same post you will receive
some New York papers from Dolby. Will you take care to send
her the Tribune? . . . I am in capital health and voice—but my
spirits flutter woefully towards a certain place at which you dined
one day not long before I left, with the present writer and a
third (most drearily missed) person.

(December 17) Enclosed, another letter "as before."

(Xmas Eve) Enclosed, another letter as before, to your protection and dispatch. I would give £3,000 down (and think it cheap) if you could forward *me,* for four and twenty hours only, instead of the letter.

(December 30) Another letter for my Darling, enclosed.

(February 21, 1868) You will have seen too (I hope) my dear Patient, and will have achieved in so doing what I would joyfully give a Thousand Guineas to achieve myself at this present moment!

(February 25) "From the same to the same." Enclosed.

(February 28) Toujours from the same to the same.

(March 16) Another letter from the same to the same.

(April 14) Enclosed, another letter to your care. By next Saturday's mail, I will send *the last!*—As there is a mail that day, I may as well forward a line by it.

(April 17—the day of departure from America) One last letter enclosed.

The reference in the letter of February 21 to "my dear Patient" might suggest that it was at this time that Ellen was expecting the child, which, according to Kate Perugini, died in infancy. However, there are other scattered references to the "Patient," all suppressed in the published letters, which make the conjecture unlikely. The term is used in letters dated as early as July 12, 1865, soon after the Staplehurst accident, seeming to indicate that Ellen suffered injuries at that time. The letter Dickens wrote to his servingman asking him to take certain delicacies to Ellen a few days after the accident has already been quoted. On July 12, 1865, Dickens wrote to Wills, "Patient immensely better." On August 16, "Patient much better, I

am thankful to say, but not yet well." And on August 25,
"Neuralgia flying about. Patient much the same." Two
years later Dickens is still using the term as an apparent
designation for Ellen; in a letter dated June 6, 1867, when
Dickens was first turning over in his mind the possibilities
of going to America, he wrote to Wills (on stationery carrying the monogram "E.T."), "The Patient I acknowledge
to be the gigantic difficulty." Again, in a note to Wills
dated July 26, 1868, he sent "all sorts of Patient Messages"
to Wills and his wife, and even as late as January 23, 1870,
not long before he died, Dickens wrote to Wills, "The
patient was in attendance [at the reading of "Nancy and
Sykes"] and missed you. I was charged with all manner of
good and kind remembrance." [16] The term may have been
continued after the Staplehurst accident as a pet designation, or simply as a mutually understood code reference
for Ellen.

In earlier letters to Wills there are passages, omitted
from all published versions, which may hint at the beginning of Dickens's infatuation for Ellen. The letters were
written in September, 1857, soon after the performance of
The Frozen Deep, in which Dickens played the part of
Richard Wardour and Ellen a minor part. "But Lord bless
you," wrote Dickens, "the strongest parts of your present
correspondent's heart are made up of weaknesses, and he
just come to be here at all (if you knew it) along of his
Richard Wardour! Guess that riddle, Mr. Wills!" Two
days later he confessed, "I am going to take the little—
riddle—into the country this morning; and I answer your
letter briefly, before starting. . . . So let the riddle and the
riddler go their own wild way, and no harm come of it!" [17]
A close reading of the text of The Frozen Deep would

reveal many lines which take on special meaning when
one remembers the dragon's teeth being sown during those
Manchester rehearsals—such lines, for example, as Wardour's, "The only hopeless wretchedness in this world is
the wretchedness that women cause." [18]

5

Decanonization

"WE HAVE HAD too many honeysuckle lives of Milton," remarked gruff, truth-loving Dr. Johnson. And again, "If a man is to write a *Panegyrick* he may Keep Vices out of sight; but if he proposes to write *A Life* he must represent it as it really was." It is to free Dickens from the panegyrists that this review of the evidence supporting the Ternan story has been presented. The panegyrists have done no service to Dickens; they have choked his genius and stifled his humanity. Of all the great figures of English literary history, Dickens has received the least serious study, because no scholar could touch him without the feeling that he was dealing with a figure out of Mrs. Jarley's waxwork. One needs only to look at some of the more recent critical studies of Dickens by scholars who have reëxamined his life and work in the light of the Ternan relationship to see the stature Dickens is able to attain when the critic is allowed to discard suppression, distortion, and myth, and to work with facts.[1] Lord Acton once remarked that Dickens knew nothing of sin when it was not a crime, but the remark applies only to the earlier novels. Recent studies of the later novels reveal the deeper knowledge of men found in them and point to Dickens's maturity under the spiritual tragedy of his later years. It is not until his later novels that Dickens portrays men who are both innocent and wicked, rather than wholly good or

59

bad. His women characters, too, become much more than
the cardboard figures of the early works. To study the
reasons for the greater maturity and depth of Dickens's
later novels is to come closer to an understanding not of
Dickens alone, but of the mysterious and delicate balance
between strength and weakness, good and bad, light and
darkness, in life itself.

These recent critical studies stand in sharp contrast to
the pretty, sentimental books containing anecdotes of how
little girls, meeting Dickens on the street, ran back exclaim-
ing delightedly, "Oh, mummy! mummy! it is Charles
Dickens," or quoting Dickens's own favorite bit of pious
fantasia about the man or woman or child who stopped him
in the streets to ask, "Mr. Dickens, will you let me touch
the hand that has filled my home with so many friends?"
The contrast illuminates the difference between Johnson's
Panegyrick and *A Life*. Chesterton pointed out long ago
what little need Dickens has of the dubious services of his
self-elected defenders, when he wrote, "Dickens has escaped from the Anti-Dickensians; with all humanity it
might also be hinted that Dickens has escaped from the
Dickensians." [2]

In a letter to Forster discussing one of the latter's
books, Dickens once wrote: "The evidence has been suppressed and coloured, and the judge goes through it and
puts it straight. It is not *his* fault if it all goes one way and
tends to one plain conclusion. Nor is it his fault that it
goes the further when it is laid out straight, or seems to do
so, because it was so knotted and twisted up before." [3]
It is hoped that the Ternan case has here "been laid out
straight." All evidence has been admitted—from the flimsi-
est gossip to the testimony of original manuscripts—in the

attempt to present as exhaustive a review of the events, both rumored and actual, as is possible at this writing. The case now rests: not the case for a sensational unmasking of Dickens, because that at no time has been the intention, but the case for establishing as true or false the allegation that Dickens and Ellen Ternan were lovers. Only that story has been reviewed here.

The Ternan episode is only one part of the whole Dickens story, however. Many more aspects of his life and character must be reviewed before anything like the whole man that was Dickens emerges from the "shadows, clouds, and darkness." That review will be the task of the biographers when they have sifted the thousands of his extant letters in which the true life of a man is contained; as Newman once remarked, "Biographers varnish, they assign motives, they conjecture feelings, they interpret Lord Burleigh's nod, but contemporary letters are facts." Not just some of the letters need to be reviewed, not just the newly discovered ones, or the most sensational. We must remember Dickens's own warning about those written "in the heat of the moment." But the accumulation of letters over the years to all sorts of people under all sorts of conditions is a much more reliable key to an understanding of the man who wrote them than are his works, even though readers do persist in taking the attitude of the critic who was shocked that Byron could have used the same penful of ink to write, "Adieu, adieu, my Native Land!" and "Huzza! Hodgson, we are going!"

This plea for the decanonization of Dickens has been made with the conviction that the restoration of his true character and personality, however imperfect they may have been, will add more to his stature as both man and writer than all the extravagant eulogies of those who would rather idolize than understand him. Once the canonizers accept facts that are clearly and unequivocally facts, and face up to the disillusioning truth that human nature, even when it belongs to the creator of the Cratchits, is likely to be human, then only will they rediscover Dickens. Such a rediscovery will lead them into the core of one man's intense personal struggle, and they will need all their wisdom and human compassion and understanding to read that struggle aright.

For one brief moment Dickens himself drew the curtain on his own "Battle of Life" and on the reasons behind what Harriet Martineau called "the hysterical restlessness" of his later years, when he wrote Georgina after having been deeply moved by a production of Faust, "It affected me so and sounded in my ears so like a mournful echo of things that lie in my own heart." [4]

Appendix: Documents

Because of the interest and relative inaccessibility of the following documents, the full texts are given here.

The Address

[Written by Dickens as editor of *Household Words*, in which magazine it appeared on the front page of the issue of June 12, 1858; its publication had been anticipated "by request" in the London *Times* of June 7, 1858, and it was reprinted in many English and American journals.]

PERSONAL

Three-and-twenty years have passed since I entered on my present relations with the Public. They began when I was so young, that I find them to have existed for nearly a quarter of a century.

Through all that time I have tried to be as faithful to the Public as they have been to me. It was my duty never to trifle with them, or deceive them, or presume upon their favour, or do anything with it but work hard to justify it. I have always endeavoured to discharge that duty.

My conspicuous position has often made me the subject of fabulous stories and unaccountable statements. Occasionally, such things have chafed me, or even wounded me; but, I have always accepted them as the shadows inseparable from the light of my notoriety and success. I have never obtruded any such personal uneasiness of mine, upon the generous aggregate of my audience.

For the first time in my life, and I believe for the last, I now deviate from the principle I have so long observed, by presenting myself in my own Journal in my own private character, and entreating all my brethren (as they deem that they have reason to think well of me, and to know that I am a man who has ever been unaffectedly true to our common calling), to lend their aid to the dissemination of my present words.

Some domestic trouble of mine, of long-standing, on which I will make no further remark than that it claims to be respected, as being of a sacredly private nature, has lately been brought to an arrangement, which involves no anger or ill-will of any kind, and the whole origin, progress, and surrounding circumstances of which have been, throughout, within the knowledge of my children. It is amicably composed, and its details have now but to be forgotten by those concerned in it.

By some means, arising out of wickedness, or out of folly, or out of inconceivable wild chance, or out of all three, this trouble has been made the occasion of misrepresentations, most grossly false, most monstrous and most cruel—involving, not only me, but innocent persons dear to my heart, and innocent persons of whom I have no knowledge, if, indeed, they have any existence—and so widely spread that I doubt if one reader in a thousand will peruse these lines, by whom some touch of the breath of these slanders will not have passed, like an unwholesome air.

Those who know me and my nature, need no assurance under my hand that such calumnies are as irreconcileable with me, as they are, in their frantic incoherence, with one another. But there is a great multitude who know me through my writings, and who do not know me otherwise; and I cannot bear that one of them should be left in doubt, or hazard of doubt, through my poorly shrinking from taking the unusual means to which I now resort, of circulating the Truth.

I most solemnly declare, then—and this I do, both in my own name and in my wife's name—that all the lately whispered rumours touching the trouble at which I have glanced are abominably false. And that whosoever repeats one of them after this denial, will lie as wilfully and as foully as it is possible for any false witness to lie, before heaven and earth.

CHARLES DICKENS

The "Violated Letter"

[First published in the New York *Tribune*, August 16, 1858, from which it was copied and reprinted in many English and American journals.]

Tuesday, May 25, 1858

Mrs. Dickens and I have lived unhappily together for many years. Hardly anyone who has known us intimately can fail to have known that we are in all respects of character and temperament wonderfully unsuited to each other. I suppose that no two people, not vicious in themselves, ever were joined together who had a greater difficulty in understanding one another, or who had less in common. An attached woman servant (more friend to both of us than a servant), who lived with us sixteen years, and is now married, and who was, and still is in Mrs. Dickens's confidence and in mine, who had the closest familiar experience of this unhappiness, in London, in the country, in France, in Italy, wherever we have been, year after year, month after month, week after week, day after day, will bear testimony to this.

Nothing has, on many occasions, stood between us and a separation but Mrs. Dickens's sister, Georgina Hogarth. From the age of fifteen she has devoted herself to our house and our children. She has been their playmate, nurse, instructress, friend, protectress, adviser and companion. In the manly consideration towards Mrs. Dickens which I owe to my wife, I will merely remark of her that the peculiarity of her character has thrown all the children on someone else. I do not know—I cannot by any stretch of fancy imagine—what would have become of them but for this aunt, who has grown up with them, to whom they are devoted, and who has sacrificed the best part of her youth and life to them. She has remonstrated, reasoned, suffered and toiled, again and again to prevent a separation between Mrs. Dickens and me. Mrs. Dickens has often expressed to her her sense of her affectionate care and devotion in the house—never more strongly than within the last twelve months.

For some years past, Mrs. Dickens has been in the habit of representing to me that it would be better for her to go away and live apart; that her always increasing estrangement made a mental disorder under which she sometimes labours —more, that she felt herself unfit for the life she had to lead as my wife, and that she would be better far away. I have uniformly replied that we must bear our misfortune, and fight the fight out to the end; that the children were the first consideration, and that I feared they must bind us together "in appearance."

At length, within these three weeks, it was suggested to me by Forster that even for their sakes, it would surely be better to reconstruct and rearrange their unhappy home. I empowered him to treat with Mrs. Dickens, as the friend of both of us for one-and-twenty years. Mrs. Dickens wished to add, on her part, Mark Lemon, and did so. On Saturday last Lemon wrote to Forster that Mrs. Dickens "gratefully and thankfully accepted" the terms I proposed to her. Of the pecuniary part of them, I will only say that I believe they are as generous as if Mrs. Dickens were a lady of distinction and I a man of fortune. The remaining parts of them are easily described—my eldest boy to live with Mrs. Dickens and take care of her; my eldest girl to keep my house; both my girls, and all my children but the eldest son, to live with me, in the continued companionship of their aunt Georgina, for whom they have all the tenderest affection that I have ever seen among young people, and who has a higher claim (as I have often declared for many years) upon my affection, respect and gratitude than anybody in the world.

I hope that no one who may become acquainted with what I write here, can possibly be so cruel and unjust, as to put any misconstruction on our separation, so far. My elder children all understand it perfectly, and all accept it as inevitable. There is not a shadow of doubt or concealment among us—my eldest son and I are one, as to it all.

Two wicked persons who should have spoken very differently of me in consideration of earned respect and gratitude, have (as I am told, and indeed to my personal knowledge) coupled with this separation the name of a young lady for whom I have great attachment and regard. I will not repeat her name—I honour it too much. Upon my soul and honour, there is not on this earth a more virtuous and spotless creature than that young lady. I know her to be innocent and pure, and as good as my own dear daughters. Further, I am quite sure that Mrs. Dickens, having received this assurance from me, must now believe it, in the respect I know her to have for me, and in the perfect confidence I know her in her better moments to repose in my truthfulness.

On this head, again, there is not a shadow of doubt or concealment between my children and me. All is open and plain among us, as though we were brothers and sisters. They are perfectly certain that I would not deceive them, and the confidence among us is without a fear.

C. D.

It having been stated to us that in reference to the differences which have resulted in the separation of Mr. and Mrs. Charles Dickens, certain statements have been circulated that such differences are occasioned by circumstances deeply affecting the moral character of Mr. Dickens and compromising the reputation and good name of others, we solemnly declare that we now disbelieve such statements. We know that they are not believed by Mrs. Dickens, and we pledge ourselves on all occasions to contradict them, as entirely destitute of foundation.

[Here follow the signatures of Mrs. Hogarth and her youngest daughter, Helen Hogarth.]

The Will of Charles Dickens

I, CHARLES DICKENS, of Gadshill Place, Higham in the county of Kent, hereby revoke all my former Wills and Codicils and declare this to be my last Will and Testament. I

give the sum of £1000 free of legacy duty to Miss Ellen Lawless Ternan, late of Houghton Place, Ampthill Square, in the
county of Middlesex. I GIVE the sum of £19 19 0 to my faithful servant Mrs. Anne Cornelius. I GIVE the sum of £19 19 0
to the daughter and only child of the said Mrs. Anne Cornelius. I GIVE the sum of £19 19 0 to each and every domestic
servant, male and female, who shall be in my employment
at the time of my decease, and shall have been in my employment for a not less period of time than one year. I GIVE the
sum of £1000 free of legacy duty to my daughter Mary
Dickens. I also give to my said daughter an annuity of £300
a year, during her life, if she shall so long continue unmarried;
such annuity to be considered as accruing from day to day,
but to be payable half yearly, the first of such half yearly
payments to be made at the expiration of six months next
after my decease. If my said daughter Mary shall marry, such
annuity shall cease; and in that case, but in that case only,
my said daughter shall share with my other children in the
provision hereinafter made for them. I GIVE to my dear sister-
in-law Georgina Hogarth the sum of £8000 free of legacy
duty. I also give to the said Georgina Hogarth all my personal
jewellery not hereinafter mentioned, and all the little familiar
objects from my writing-table and my room, and she will
know what to do with those things. I ALSO GIVE to the said
Georgina Hogarth all my private papers whatsoever and
wheresoever, and I leave her my grateful blessings as the
best and truest friend man ever had. I GIVE to my eldest son
Charles my library of printed books, and my engravings and
prints; and I also give to my son Charles the silver salver
presented to me at Birmingham, and the silver cup presented
to me at Edinburgh, and my shirt studs, shirt pins, and sleeve
buttons. AND I BEQUEATH unto my said son Charles and my
son Henry Fielding Dickens, the sum of £8000 upon trust
to invest the same, and from time to time to vary the investments thereof, and to pay the annual income thereof to my
wife during her life, and after her decease the said sum of
£8000 and the investments thereof shall be in trust for my

children (but subject as to my daughter Mary to the proviso hereinbefore contained) who being a son or sons shall have attained or shall attain the age of twenty-one years, or being a daughter or daughters shall have attained or shall attain that age or be previously married, in equal shares if more than one. I GIVE my watch (the gold repeater presented to me at Coventry), and I give the chains and seals and all appendages I have worn with it, to my dear and trusty friend John Forster, of Palace Gate House, Kensington, in the county of Middlesex aforesaid; and I also give to the said John Forster such manuscripts of my published works as may be in my possession at the time of my decease. AND I DEVISE AND BEQUEATH all my real and personal estate (except such as is vested in me as a trustee or mortgagee) unto the said Georgina Hogarth and the said John Forster, their heirs, executors, administrators, and assigns respectively, upon trust that they the said Georgina Hogarth and John Forster, or the survivor of them or the executors or administrators of such survivor, do and shall, at their, his, or her uncontrolled and irresponsible direction, either proceed to an immediate sale or conversion into money of the said real or personal estate (including my copyrights), or defer and postpone any sale or conversion into money, till such time or times as they, he, or she shall think fit, and in the meantime may manage and let the said real and personal estate (including my copyrights), in such manner in all respects as I myself could do, if I were living and acting therein; it being my intention that the trustees or trustee for the time being of this my will shall have the fullest power over the said real and personal estate which I can give to them, him, or her. AND I DECLARE that, until the said real and personal estate shall be sold and converted into money, the rents and annual income thereof respectively shall be paid and applied to the person or persons in the manner and for the purposes to whom and for which the annual income of the monies to arise from the sale or conversion thereof into money would be payable or applicable under this my Will in case the same were sold or converted into money. AND I DECLARE that my real estate shall for the purposes of this my Will be considered as converted into personalty upon my decease. AND I DECLARE that the said trustees or trustee for the time being, do and shall, with and out of the monies which shall come to their, his, or her hands, under or by virtue of this my Will and the trusts thereof, pay my just debts, funeral and testamentary expenses, and legacies. AND I DECLARE that the said trust funds or so much thereof as shall remain after answering the purposes aforesaid, and the annual income thereof, shall be in trust for all my children (but subject as to my daughter Mary to the proviso hereinbefore contained), who being a son or sons shall have attained or shall attain the age of twenty-one years, and being a daughter or daughters shall have attained or shall attain that age or be previously married, in equal shares if more than one. PROVIDED ALWAYS, that, as regards my copyrights and the produce and profits thereof, my said daughter Mary, notwithstanding the proviso hereinbefore contained with reference to her, shall share with my other children therein whether she be married or not. AND I DEVISE the estates vested in me at my decease as a trustee or mortgagee unto the use of the said Georgina Hogarth and John Forster, their heirs and assigns, upon the trusts and subject to the equities affecting the same respectively. AND I APPOINT the said GEORGINA HOGARTH and JOHN FORSTER executrix and executor of this my Will, and GUARDIANS of the persons of my children during their respective minorities. AND LASTLY, as I have now set down the form of words which my legal advisors assure me are necessary to the plain objects of this my Will, I solemnly enjoin my dear children always to remember how much they owe to the said Georgina Hogarth, and never to be wanting in a grateful and affectionate attachment to her, for they know well that she has been, through all the stages of their growth and progress, their ever useful self-denying and devoted friend. AND I DESIRE here simply to record the fact that my wife, since our separation by consent, has been in the receipt from me of an annual income of £600, while all the great charges of a numerous and expensive family have devolved wholly upon myself. I emphatically direct that I be buried in an inexpensive, unostentatious, and strictly private manner; that no public announcement be made of the time or place of my burial; that at the utmost not more than three plain mourning coaches be employed; and that those who attend my funeral wear no scarf, cloak, black bow, long hatband, or other such revolting absurdity. I DIRECT that my name be inscribed in plain English letters on my tomb, without the addition of "Mr." or "Esquire." I conjure my friends on no account to make me the subject of any monument, memorial, or testimonial whatever. I rest my claims to the remembrance of my country upon my published works, and to the remembrance of my friends upon their experience of me in addition thereto. I commit my soul to the mercy of God through our Lord and Saviour Jesus Christ, and I exhort my dear children humbly to try to guide themselves by the teaching of the New Testament in its broad spirit, and to put no faith in any man's narrow construction of its letter here or there. IN WITNESS whereof I the said Charles Dickens, the testator, have to this my last Will and Testament set my hand this 12th day of May in the year of our Lord 1869.

CHARLES DICKENS.

Signed published and declared by the above-named Charles Dickens the testator as and for his last Will and Testament in the presence of us (present together at the same time) who in his presence at his request and in the presence of each other have hereunto subscribed our names as witnesses.

G. HOLSWORTH,
26 Wellington Street, Strand.
HENRY WALKER,
26 Wellington Street, Strand.

I, CHARLES DICKENS of Gadshill Place near Rochester in the county of Kent Esquire declare this to be a Codicil to my last Will and Testament which Will bears date of 12th day of May 1869. I GIVE to my son Charles Dickens the

younger all my share and interest in the weekly journal called "All the Year Round," which is now conducted under Articles of Partnership made between me and William Henry Wills and the said Charles Dickens the younger, and all my share and interest in the stereotypes, stock and other effects belonging to the said partnership, he defraying my share of all debts and liabilities of the said partnership which may be outstanding at the time of my decease, and in all other respects I confirm my said Will. IN WITNESS whereof I have hereunto set my hand the 2nd day of June in the year of our Lord 1870.
CHARLES DICKENS.

Signed and declared by the said CHARLES DICKENS, the testator as and for a Codicil to his Will in the presence of us present at the same time who at his request in his presence and in the presence of each other hereunto subscribe our names as witnesses.
G. HOLSWORTH,
26 Wellington Street, Strand.
HENRY WALKER,
26 Wellington Street, Strand.

Statement of Bradbury and Evans, Publishers of "Household Words"

[First published before the text of number 20 of the monthly parts of Thackeray's *The Virginians*, June, 1859.]

Their connection with *Household Words* ceased *against their will*, under circumstances of which the following are material:
So far back as 1836, Bradbury & Evans had business relations with Mr. Dickens, and, in 1844, an agreement was entered into, by which they acquired an interest in all the works he might write, or in any periodical he might originate, during a term of seven years. Under this agreement Bradbury & Evans became possessed of a joint, though unequal, interest with Mr. Dickens in *Household Words* commenced in 1850. Friendly relations had simultaneously sprung up between

them, and they were on terms of close intimacy in 1858, when circumstances led to Mr. Dickens's publication of a statement on the subject of his conjugal differences, in various newspapers, including *Household Words* of June 12th.

The public disclosure of these differences took most persons by surprise, and was notoriously the subject of comments, by no means complimentary to Mr. Dickens himself, as regarded the taste of this proceeding. On the 17th of June, however, Bradbury & Evans learned, from a common friend, that Mr. Dickens had resolved to break off his connection with them, because this statement was not printed in the number of *Punch* published the day preceding—in other words, because it did not occur to Bradbury & Evans to exceed their legitimate functions as proprietors and publishers, and to require the insertion of statements on a domestic and painful subject, in the inappropriate columns of a comic miscellany. No previous request for the insertion of this statement had been made either to Bradbury & Evans, or to the editor of *Punch,* and the grievance of Mr. Dickens substantially amounted to this, that Bradbury & Evans did not take upon themselves, unsolicited, to gratify an eccentric wish by a preposterous action.

Mr. Dickens, with ample time for reflection, persisted in the attitude he had taken up, and in the following November, summoned a meeting of the proprietors of *Household Words.* He did not himself attend this meeting; but a literary friend of Mr. Dickens came to it as his representative, and announced there, officially, that Mr. Dickens, in consequence of the non-appearance, in *Punch,* of his statement, considered that Bradbury & Evans had shown such disrespect and want of good faith towards him, as to determine him, in so far as he had the power, to disconnect himself from them in business transactions; and the friend above mentioned, on the part of Mr. Dickens, accordingly moved a resolution dissolving the partnership, and discontinuing the work on May 28. Bradbury & Evans replied that they did not and could not believe that this was the sole cause of Mr. Dickens's altered feeling towards them; but they were assured that it was the sole cause, and that Mr. Dickens desired to bear testimony to their integrity and zeal as his publishers, but that his resolution was formed, and nothing would alter it. Bradbury & Evans repeatedly pressed Mr. Dickens's friend upon this point, but with no other result.

Thus, on this ground alone, Mr. Dickens puts an end to personal and business relations of long standing; and by an unauthorized and premature public announcement of the cessation of *Household Words,* he forced Bradbury & Evans to an unwilling recourse to the Court of Chancery to restrain him from such proceedings, thereby injuring a valuable property in which others beside himself were interested. In fact, by this mode of proceeding he inflicted as much injury as his opportunities afforded. Not having succeeded in purchasing the share of his partners at his own price, he depreciated the value of this share by all the agencies at his command. By publicly announcing (so far as the Court of Chancery permitted) his intention to discontinue the publication of *Household Words;* by advertising a second work of a similar class under his management, by producing it, and by making it as close an imitation as was legally safe of *Household Words,* while that publication was actually still issuing, and still conducted by him; he took a course calculated to reduce the circulation and impair the prospects of a common property; and if he inflicted this injury on his partners, it is no compensation to them that he simultaneously sacrificed his own interest in the publication he is about to suppress.

Household Words having been sold on the 16th inst., under a decree in Chancery, Bradbury & Evans have no further interest in its continuance, and are now free to make this personal statement, and to associate themselves in the establishment of *Once a Week.*

Notes

1. Household Saint

[1] London *Figaro*, June 10, 1870, p. 1.

[2] *Dante Gabriel Rossetti, His Family-Letters. With a Memoir by William Michael Rossetti* (London, 1895), I, 289.

[3] June 17, 1870.

[4] The Rev. Dr. Child, quoted in the New York *Tribune*, July 12, 1870.

[5] William Rounseville Alger. *The Sword, the Pen, and the Pulpit; with a Tribute to the Christian Genius and Memory of Charles Dickens. A Discourse Delivered in Boston Music Hall, on Sunday, June 19, 1870* (Boston, 1870).

[6] *Whither Bound? A Sermon Occasioned by the Canonization of Charles Dickens* (Boston, 1870).

[7] The Rev. Lemuel Moss, quoted in the appendix of Fulton's *Whither Bound*, p. 31.

[8] *Charles Dickens: A Biographical and Critical Study* (London, 1950), in his prefatory note and *passim*.

[9] See especially Wagenknecht's "Dickens and the Scandal-mongers," *College English*, XI, 373–382 (April, 1950), and T. W. Hill's "Dickensian Biography from Forster to the Present Day" (Part II), *Dickensian*, XLVII, 72–79 (1951). See also the articles by J. W. T. Ley in the *Dickensian*, XXVI, 37–38 (1929–1930); XXXI, 226–230 (1935); XXXII, 15–21 (1935); XXXIII, 47–51, 205–211 (1936); XXXV, 250–253 (1939); and his letter to the Editor of "Books," New York *Herald Tribune*, July 5, 1936, p. 12. For a brief but pertinent and sensible objection to Wagenknecht's remarks, see Richard B. Hudson, "The Dickens Affair Again," *College English*, XIII, 111–113 (November, 1951).

[10] In a review of the third volume of Forster's *Life of Charles Dickens, Atlantic Monthly*, XXXIII, 622.

[11] *Dickensian*, XLVII, 77 (1951).

2. Ellen Ternan

[1] *Records of the New York Stage from 1750 to 1860* (New York, 1867), II, 107.

75

² George C. D. Odell, *Annals of the New York Stage* (New York, 1928), IV, 13. A list of the parts played by the Ternans in Philadelphia will be found in Arthur Herman Wilson's *A History of the Philadelphia Theatre, 1835 to 1855* (Philadelphia, 1935).

³ See the account in Malcolm Morley, "Theatre Royal, Montreal," *Dickensian*, XLV, 39 (1948–1949); also *Diaries of William Charles Macready* (ed. William Toynbee), II, 347.

⁴ *Diaries of William Charles Macready*, I, 111.

⁵ *Ibid.*, II, 348.

⁶ *Ibid.*, II, 313.

⁷ Walter Dexter, ed., *The Letters of Charles Dickens* (Bloomsbury, Eng.: Nonesuch Press, 1938), II, 877. This edition of the letters will be used throughout these notes.

⁸ Letter to Mrs. Richard Watson, December 7, 1857, quoted in Franklin P. Rolfe, "More Letters to the Watsons," *Dickensian*, XXXVIII, 190 (Autumn, 1942); the original MS is in the Huntington Library.

⁹ Such as in the letter to the theatrical manager, Benjamin Webster: "I have a high opinion of the young lady and take a strong interest in herself and her family. It is likely enough that you know what she can do—how that she is accomplished and attractive, well used to the stage, sings prettily, and is favorably known to London audiences. If you should be undecided between two applicants of equal pretensions (counting this young lady as one), I should be heartily glad if you would turn the scale in my direction—as I am sure you would in any such case." (*Letters*, III, 235.) Another to Edmund Yates expresses the wish that "Fechter would take among his young ladies Miss Maria Ternan. Not because I have a great friendship for her and know her to be one of the best and bravest of little spirits and most virtuous of girls (for that would have nothing to do with it), but because I have acted with her, and believe her to have more aptitude in a minute than all the other people of her standing on the stage in a month. A lady besides, and pretty, and of a good figure, and always painstaking and perfect to the letter. Also (but this has never had a chance) a wonderful mimic. Whatever he shewed her, she would do. When I first knew her, I looked her in the eyes one morning at Manchester, and she took the whole Frozen Deep out of the look and six words." (*Letters*, III, 291.) See also Dickens's long accounts of her acting with him in *The Frozen Deep* in the letter to Miss Coutts of September 5, 1857 (*Letters*, II, 877), and in the letter to Mrs. Watson mentioned in the preceding note.

¹⁰ Best known of her portraits is probably that of her brother-in-law, Thomas Adolphus Trollope, which was reproduced as the frontispiece in his autobiography, *What I Remember* (London, 1887).

[11] Appearances at the Olympic in 1855 and 1856 included those as: Julia in *The Welsh Girl,* Rose in *Tit for Tat,* Dolly Hardup in *Garrick Fever,* Sarah Blunt in *Poor Pillocoddy,* Princess Babillarda in *The Discreet Princess,* Mrs. Benson in *To Oblige Benson,* Miss Bromley in *Perfection,* Mrs. Lauriston in *Stay at Home,* Bridget in *The Family Queen,* Orpheus in *Medea,* Luise in *The Green-Eyed Monster,* Kitty in *Shocking Events.* She also appeared as Oberon in *A Midsummer Night's Dream* with Charles Kean at the Princess Theatre, October 15, 1856. I am indebted for these listings and for other information about the theatrical careers of the Ternan family to Mr. G. W. Nash, director of the Enthoven Theatre Collection at the Victoria and Albert Museum.

[12] See later account of this letter, and of Frances Eleanor, pp. 50 ff.

[13] On August 19, 1867, less than a year after the marriage, Browning, a devoted friend of Tom Trollope's, wrote to Isa Blagden about rumors of a quarrel and separation over "revelations of the past misfortunes of which T. had been ignorant altogether" (*Dearest Isa: Robert Browning's Letters to Isabella Blagden,* ed. Edward C. McAleer. University of Texas Press, Austin, 1951, p. 277). The separation did not take place, however, and during his brother's illness some years later Anthony Trollope was able to write his sister-in-law: "I cannot tell you the admiration I have for you. Your affection and care and assiduity were to be expected. I knew you well enough to take them as a matter of course from you to him. But your mental and physical capacity, your power of sustaining him by your own cheerfulness, and supporting him by your own attention, are marvellous. When I consider all the circumstances, I hardly know how to reconcile so much love with so much self-control." (Thomas Adolphus Trollope, *What I Remember,* II, 325 f.)

[14] *The Autobiography of Alfred Austin, Poet Laureate, 1835–1910* (London, 1911), I, 209. The Austins had been invited to the Villa Trollope as "chaperones" for Tom and his new governess.

[15] *Aunt Margaret's Trouble* ran in *All the Year Round* from July 14 to August 16, 1866; although hardly long enough for a novel, it proved a popular success and went into seven editions in book form, carrying the dedication "This LITTLE STORY is affectionately dedicated to E. L. T." (i.e., Ellen Lawless Ternan). Dickens praised the story in a number of his letters and was amused that the anonymous work had been ascribed to Mrs. Brookfield. Her second and much longer novel, *Mabel's Progress,* also ran in *All the Year Round* and was afterward published as a "three-decker." It was followed by ten other novels and many articles and translations. Her facility with the Italian language prompted Pope Leo XIII to send her a special blessing

as "the lady who had spoken such remarkably pure Italian." (Lucy
Poate and Richard Poate Stebbins, *The Trollopes*, New York, 1945,
p. 324.)

[16] *Frances Trollope, Her Life and Literary Work from George
III. to Victoria*, by her daughter-in-law, Frances Eleanor Trollope
(2 vols., London, 1895).

[17] Besides the part in *Atalanta*, these included parts at the Olympic in *Garrick Fever*, June 11, 1855, and *The Discreet Princess*, April
2, 1856; at the Haymarket, as Louise in *My Son Diana*, October 17,
1857, as Mrs. Fitzherbert in *Victims*, October 26, 1857, as Mrs. Cap-
tain Phobbs in *Lend Me Five Shillings*, November 9, 1857, as Fanny
in *Take Care of Dowb*, November 23, 1857, as Margaret in *The
Dowager*, December 23, 1857, and as Susan in *Speed the Plough*,
December 28, 1857. According to E. L. Blanchard (*Life and Reminiscences*, New York, 1891, I, 210, 215), Ellen also appeared as
Alice in *The Tide of Time*, December 16, 1858, and as Lady Castle-
crag in *The World and the Stage*, March 12, 1859. She was billed to
appear at the Haymarket on August 4, 1859, as Mrs. Gatherwood in
Out of Sight Out of Mind, but on August 11 Maria Ternan is listed
in the part. This is the last recorded appearance that I have been able
to find.

[18] This story was first told by Thomas Wright in *The Life of
Charles Dickens* (New York, 1936), p. 244, but he did not give his
source. Most later biographers have picked up the story from Wright.
Wright reproduces a picture of Ellen in the part of Hippomenes (p.
249).

[19] Notice in the *Era*, April 19, 1857; quoted in Wright, *op. cit.*,
p. 249.

[20] *Letters*, II, 866.

[21] The statement had first appeared in the London *Times* on June
7, 1858 (p. 10, col. 6), with the introduction, "We are requested to
anticipate the publication of the following article.—" From the *Times*
the item was copied by a number of other English and American
journals; see, e.g., the Manchester *Guardian*, June 8, 1858, p. 3, col.
6. For the full text of the statement see the Appendix, pp. 63–67.

[22] Dickens made a point in his correspondence at this time of
explaining that Charley went with his mother at his father's express
insistence, but the letter from Charley to his father at the time he left
home seems to imply that he himself made the decision—probably in
the face of Dickens's disapproval. He wrote:

"My Dear Father,—What you told me this morning so completely
took me by surprise, that I am afraid I did not completely make myself
understood to you, and I think I can write you better what I mean
than say it to you.

"Don't suppose that in making my choice, I was actuated by any feeling of preference for my mother to you. God knows I love you dearly, and it will be a hard day for me when I have to part from you and the girls.

"But in doing as I have done, I hope I am doing my duty, and that you will understand it so.—I remain my dear Father—ever your affectionate son." (*Letters*, III, 25 n.)

Charley further stood against his father in marrying Bessie Evans, daughter of the publisher whose home was forbidden to the rest of the children, and there is clear evidence in the later letters of Georgina and of Forster that Charley was not the family favorite. When Forster was writing his biography of Dickens, it was rumored that Charley insisted that it include no disparagement of Mrs. Dickens or he himself would publish the true facts. Both Forster and Georgina were indignant at Charley's purchase (at a low bid) of Gad's Hill when it was put up for auction after Dickens's death. Dickens, however, made his peace with his son, coming to his rescue when his business venture failed, taking him on the staff of *All the Year Round*, and willing him at his death his share of stock in the magazine.

The other boys were too young to understand what was happening or to take sides. With the exception of Henry Fielding Dickens, the family favorite, and Charley, all the boys left England in their teens for Australia or for military service abroad. Alfred, who went to Australia in 1865 and did not return to England until 1910, wrote the following letter from Australia at the time of his father's death in 1870. It not only reveals how much in ignorance the younger boys were kept, but also shows a warmth of feeling for Mrs. Dickens that her husband was ever loath to recognize or acknowledge. The letter (here quoted through the kindness of Mr. K. J. Fielding, from a microfilm copy of the letter in the Melbourne Library) is addressed to G. W. Rusden and is dated August 11, 1870:

"There is but one unfortunate incident in our father's life, and that was doubtless his separation from our Mother. As people will doubtless talk about this may I ask you to state the facts properly for myself and Plorn [his younger brother, also in Australia] should they be misrepresented. When the separation took place it made no difference in our feelings toward them: we their children always loved them both equally, having free intercourse with both as of old: while not one word on the subject *ever* passed from the lips of either father or mother. Of the causes which led to this unfortunate event, we know no more than the rest of the world. Our dear mother has suffered very much. My brother's wife in her letter says—'Poor dear she is better than I dared to hope she would be, and I am sure that in a little time she will be more settled, and even happier than she

has been for years, for she says what is true that she has already
lived 12 years of widowhood and she feels that there is nobody nearer
to him than she is.'
"My heart is too full to write of any subject but this today."
    [23] Miss Gladys Storey (*Dickens and Daughter*, p. 164) records
that Georgina and her sister were reconciled after Dickens's death,
though there is no indication of how heartfelt a reconciliation it was.
That Mrs. Dickens at her death willed Georgina "the blue enamel
snake-ring given to her by Count D'Orsay," as Miss Storey relates,
might be interpreted as indicative of something other than sisterly
affection.
    [24] From a letter, dated July 11, 1858, to Miss S. Bayley, in the
Browning Collection of the University of Texas Library; quoted in
Harry Ransom, *The Brownings in Paris, 1858,* University of Texas
Studies in English, 1941, pp. 151 f.; reprinted in *Notes and Queries,*
CLXXXV, 45 (July 17, 1943).
    [25] Gordon N. Ray, ed., *The Letters and Private Papers of Wil-
liam Makepeace Thackeray* (Cambridge, Mass., 1946), IV, 87.
    [26] See the full text of the "Statement" in the Appendix.
    [27] *Fifty Years of London Life: Memoirs of a Man of the World*
(New York, 1885), p. 286.
    [28] J. W. T. Ley's edition of Forster's *Life of Charles Dickens*
(London [1928]), p. 648. In an unpublished letter to Macready,
dated June 7, 1858, the day the statement appeared in the *Times,*
Dickens wrote: "You will see that some printed words of mine were
laid on the breakfast table this morning in the Times. . . . Forster advised with Delane for an hour and a half on Saturday. And Delane
on the whole decided *in favor of the publication.* This turned the
balance, as we had settled that it should, either way." (Original
letter now at the Pierpont Morgan Library.)
    [29] Quoted in "Charles Dickens: A Critical Biography," in *Our
Contemporaries: Literary—Political—Artistic—Etc., Etc.,* No. 1 (London, 1858), p. 65.
    [30] *Ibid.,* p. 74.
    [31] Both Wright (*Life,* pp. 268, 272) and Una Pope-Hennessy
(pp. 387 f.) record that Dickens forced them to sign, holding over
them the threat that he would turn his wife out of the house without
a penny if they did not. Wright based his account on a letter from Mrs.
Dickens's aunt, Helen Thomson, to a Mrs. Stark. This letter, which
Wright could not obtain permission to publish, was dated August
20, 1858, and mentioned the threat referred to above. See Wright's
letter in the *Dickensian,* XXXII, 98 (March, 1936); also in his autobiography, *Thomas Wright of Olney* (London [1936]), p. 237.
Hugh Kingsmill, in his *The Sentimental Journey: A Life of Charles
Dickens* (London, 1934), prefatory note and pp. 183 f., also quotes

from this letter, which he states Ralph Straus showed him. For an attack upon the authenticity of the letter, see the *Dickensian*, XXXIII, 1–4 (December, 1936).

[32] *Fifty Years of London Life*, p. 288.

[33] *Letters*, III, 73.

[34] In letters to Forster (October, 1861), *Letters*, III, 243; and to Macready (October 13, 1861), *Letters*, III, 245.

[35] Charley, the eldest son, wrote his mother at his father's dictation and quoted his father's directives: "I positively forbid the children ever to utter one word to their grandmother or to Helen Hogarth. If they are ever brought into the presence of either of these two, I charge them immediately to leave your mother's house and come back to me." And in reference to Mark Lemon, "I positively forbid the children ever to see him or to speak to him and for the same reason I absolutely prohibit their ever being taken to Mr. Evans's house." (Quoted in *Mr. & Mrs. Charles Dickens: His Letters to Her*, with a Foreword by their daughter Kate Perugini and Notes, Appendices, etc., by Walter Dexter, London, 1935, p. 280.) The original of this letter is in the Huntington Library.

At the time of the separation Dickens had written to Evans, who later was to become Charley's father-in-law: "Dear Sir,—I have had stern occasion to impress upon my children that their father's name is their best possession and that it would indeed be trifled with and wasted by him, if, either through himself or through them, he held any terms with those who have been false to it, in the only great need and under the only great wrong it has ever known. You know very well, why (with hard distress of mind and bitter disappointment), I have been forced to include you in this class. I have no more to say." (*Letters*, III, 33.)

[36] Dickens had written Mary Boyle one of his long letters of explanation asking her to "circulate the truth" about his separation; after receiving her sympathetic answer, Dickens wrote Georgina: "I had a letter from 'Meery' [his pen name for her] at York, which I answered. Very affectionate! But really sincere and earnest." (*Letters*, III, 54.) There is an interesting series of letters from Dickens to Mary Boyle, most of them unpublished, at the Morgan Library. She, like Ellen, acted with Dickens in amateur theatricals, though she was much nearer his own age. The letters show a gradual increase in intimacy from "My Dear Miss Boyle" (in 1850) to "Beloved Mary" (in 1856). Their chief interest here is that they indicate something of Dickens's restless dissatisfaction with the domestic hearth *before* he fell in love with Ellen; there is a noticeable cooling off in the letters after Dickens met Ellen in 1857. An early letter to Mary, dated January 15, 1851, and written from the "Loft over Stable," is a special revelation of Dickens's state of mind in the pre-Ellen days:

"I am like the man in the play—do you know the drama?—in five acts—sentimental comedy—virtue in distress—lovely woman—and all that—well! Like that man, the call of honor stands between me and my rest—baulks my inclination—beckons me from happiness—to the regions (do you understand, my angel?) of state formality &c &c. . . . To stay here, tomorrow, would be most delightful to me—but would be too much pepper—I mean happiness. I have learnt a good lesson. A man's happiness, after all, don't depend upon himself. With employment for the mind—exercise for the body—a domestic hearth—and a cheerful spirit—there may be many things wanting to complete his happiness—and he may be confoundedly miserable." Five years later, writing to complain of the wretchedness of suffering from a bad cold, Dickens exclaims, "Then it is my dear that I wish you were with me, occupying Tavistock House and forgetting mankind."

³⁷ Dated June 19, 1858 (a week after the appearance of the article which gave offense to Thackeray); reprinted in the *Dickensian*, XXXV, 91 (1939). After several sentences of enthusiastic praise, Yates wrote: "A domestic matter, with which the general public cannot have the slightest concern, and into which it is clearly not our province to enter, has given occasion for the fabrication of certain lies, so preposterous in their malice, as almost to defeat the design of their concocters; but the very nature of which, involving as it did the name of most innocent and worthy persons, demanded instant denial. This denial Mr. Dickens has made in a most solemn and earnest public statement, a statement breathing truth in every line."

³⁸ *Letters*, III, 74.

³⁹ Thackeray, *Letters*, IV, 86–87.

⁴⁰ The Morgan Library is in possession of a series of letters written to Mrs. Dickens after the separation which present a pathetic picture of her attempts to keep alive some contact, however remote, with her famous husband; many are responses to her requests for copies of his latest books, or tickets to dramatizations of his novels.

⁴¹ See K. J. Fielding, "Charles Dickens and Colin Rae Brown," *Nineteenth-Century Fiction*, VII, 103–110 (September, 1952).

⁴² Thackeray, *Letters*, IV, 83-84.

⁴³ Dated from London, Wednesday, June 8, 1858.

⁴⁴ October 23 [1870?]; from collection of newspaper clippings at the Antiquarian Library, Worcester, Massachusetts.

⁴⁵ *Retrospections of an Active Life*, IV, 383.

3. A Half Century of Rumor

¹ *Gossip of the Century*, by the author of "Flemish Interiors," "De Omnibus Rebus," &c. (New York, 1892), I, 225-226.

2 The diary is in the possession of the Massachusetts Historical Society; the entry is dated November 28, 1867.

3 I, 264. The actress seen by Bigelow may have been Maria, not Ellen Ternan, however. According to the records in the Enthoven Collection at the Victoria and Albert Museum, Maria was playing at the Haymarket from April 25, 1859, to June 25, 1860, but there is no record of Ellen's appearance there after August 4, 1859.

4 P. 53.

5 Letters, III, 429, 424. In a recent issue of the Dickensian (XLVII, 77), Mr. T. W. Hill calls in question the presence of Ellen at the Staplehurst accident, using a passage from a letter of Sir Arthur Sullivan as part of his refutation. An account of Sullivan's rushing about Paris with Dickens just before the accident, which occurred when Dickens was returning from this Paris visit, prompts Hill to wonder what Dickens did with Ellen and her mother during all the rushing about. The letter as given in Arthur Lawrence's Sir Arthur Sullivan: Life Story, Letters and Reminiscences (Chicago and New York, 1900), p. 52, reads: "We called upon Dickens, and then all dined together (the Dickens, Lehmanns, and selves) at the Cafe Brébant." The phrase "the Dickens" (Hill chooses to quote B. W. Findon's altered version [Sir Arthur Sullivan and His Operas, London, 1908, p. 48]: "the Lehmanns, Dickens, and selves") in the absence of a Mrs. Dickens would seem to indicate a companion accepted as part of his family.

6 CLXV, 87 (August 5, 1933).

7 Some Reminiscences of William Michael Rossetti (New York, 1906), I, 100.

8 The Journal of Benjamin Moran, 1857–1865, ed. Sarah Agnes Wallace and Frances Elma Gillespie (University of Chicago Press, 1948), I, 344: square brackets as in text.

9 Dearest Isa, pp. 348 f.

10 Arnold Quamoclit, "Charles Dickens as a Humaniser," St. James's Magazine, XLIV, 281.

11 Phrenological Journal (New York), LI, 104 (August, 1870).

12 The play, Dickens, A Comedy, of which no printed copy has been located, was first discussed in 1895 in the Melbourne Imperial Revue; this account is referred to in the introduction to S. T. Adair Fitzgerald's Dickens and the Drama. See the discussion in "Mr. John Garraway's 'Precious Comedy,'" Dickensian, XLVII, 49–50 (December, 1950).

13 Manchester Evening News, September 16, 1893; quoted in Wright, Life, p. 283.

14 The Life and Adventures of George Augustus Sala, Written by Himself (New York, 1895), I, 318.

15 Fifty Years of London Life, p. 287.

[16] *My Literary Life,* with a Prefatory Note by Miss Beatrice Harraden (London, 1899), pp. 61, 63–64; also quoted in *Notes and Queries,* CLXXXIV, 216 (April 10, 1943).

[17] *Fifty Years of London Life,* p. 285.

[18] "Charles Dickens as a Husband," *Bookman,* XXXIV, 626.

[19] Unpublished letter to John Overs, October 27, 1841; Berg Collection, New York Public Library.

[20] A number of letters in the Nonesuch edition tell of the burning of letters; see III, 177, 231, 416, 778. Miss Gladys Storey, describing the burning of a great pile of correspondence on September 3, 1860, records that Dickens remarked as the last basketful of letters was thrown on the fire: "Would to God every letter I had ever written was on that pile" (*Dickens and Daughter,* p. 107). When Dickens told John Bigelow that he had burned great quantities of letters from Sydney Smith, Bigelow "told him that he deserved to have been burned with them" (*Retrospections,* IV, 128).

[21] According to Thomas Wright, a packet of letters from Dickens to Ellen was offered for sale in London in 1893. He had the story from W. R. Hughes, who said he advised the vendor to "go home and burn them." (*Life of Charles Dickens,* p. 282.) Nothing has been heard of the letters since.

[22] When certain letters of Dickens to his wife which have been omitted from all published collections, even the Nonesuch, were published in 1935 in the volume, *Mr. & Mrs. Charles Dickens: His Letters to Her,* they were introduced by the following statement by Dickens's daughter, Kate Perugini: "Shortly before my mother's death in 1879, she placed in my hands the letters written to her by my father, before and after their marriage. She wished me to do with them as I might think best, only stipulating that, at some future date, they should be made public. They would show the world, she said, that my father had once loved her; and would make it apparent that the separation which took place between them in 1858, was not owing to any fault on her side." In this connection, see G. B. Shaw's letter to the editor of *Time and Tide,* July 27, 1935 (p. 1111), in which he claims credit for opening Kate's eyes "to the fact that there was a case for her mother as well as her father," and for advising her not to destroy these letters.

[23] Huntington Library MS.

[24] In recent years a block of the early letters to Forster has been turned over to the Victoria and Albert Museum, but the letters from 1840 on are still missing. The story goes that for the last volume or volumes of the *Life* Forster pasted portions of the original letters to his manuscript; the story has not been verified, as the manuscript has disappeared.

[25] Dated May 7, 1873; original at the Victoria and Albert Museum.

[26] As an answer to Wright's attackers, who had charged that the alleged revelations of Canon Benham were complete falsifications, a facsimile of Benham's letter containing this information was reproduced in Wright's posthumous autobiography, *Thomas Wright of Olney: An Autobiography* (London, 1936), p. 66. In the letter, Canon Benham says that he is "very glad you are going to publish a life of Dickens," and then refers to Ellen as "the lady concerning whom he quarrelled with his wife." For further remonstrances against Wright's detractors, see Mrs. Wright's statements in *Notes and Queries*, CLXXXV, 111 (August 14, 1943).

[27] See *Dickensian*, XXX, 47 (1936); also Wagenknecht, *College English*, XI, 376 (April, 1950).

[28] T. W. Hill, in the *Dickensian*, XLVII, 73.

[29] Account given in a personal letter from Miss Storey to the writer, dated July 25, 1951; substantially the same account is given in a letter from Walter Dexter to Professor Franklin P. Rolfe, which I have seen but have no permission to publish.

[30] Miss Storey in the letter mentioned above.

[31] P. 91.

[32] P. 94.

[33] Pp. 93 f.

[34] P. 219.

[35] This has been the most warmly challenged of Miss Storey's statements. That no birth certificate has been found does not, as some suggest, make the statement improbable, since registry of illegitimate births was not a legal requirement at the time. Wright went further than Miss Storey and, in letters to Walter Dexter and to J. W. T. Ley, stated: "There were children." (See Ley's statements in the *Dickensian*, XXXIII, 48, 51 [December, 1936].) At the time of his death Wright was following up clues relating to the identity of a child who did not die in infancy. If it is true that a child survived, the fact of survival would account for the intense secrecy which has always been observed in connection with the Dickens-Ternan story.

[36] P. 94.

[37] Literary Supplement of the London *Times* July 29, 1939, p. 453. Shaw had written earlier, in his preface to the edition of *Great Expectations* published by the Limited Editions Club (Edinburgh, 1937): "Dickens, when he let himself go in Great Expectations, was separated from his wife and free to make more intimate acquaintances with women than a domesticated man can. I know nothing of his adventures in this phase of his career, though I daresay a good deal of it will be dug out by the little sect of anti-Dickensites whose

fanaticism has been provoked by the Dickens Fellowships, and threatens to become as pathological as Bacon-Shakespear. It is not necessary to suggest a love affair; for Dickens could get from a passing glance a hint which he could expand into a full-grown character." (P. xix.) Mr. Wagenknecht has used this earlier statement as evidence that Shaw supported his side of the argument (see *College English*, XI, 379 n.), ignoring the later and unequivocal statement in the *Times* Literary Supplement.

[38] *Dickensian*, XXXV, 30 (1938–1939).

[39] Others, strangely enough, which had been correctly printed in what the present editors of the projected new edition of letters refer to as "the Mamie-Georgie" edition, or in other printed versions, appear in altered or garbled form in the Nonesuch. Paragraphs out of one letter appear in another of a different year, addressed to a different person; dates are wrong (even though perfectly plain in the original). Where Dickens speaks of the suicide of Henry Bradbury, son of the publisher, the Mamie-Georgie edition omits the paragraph, the Lehmann edition of the Dickens-Wills correspondence leaves the name blank, and the Nonesuch *supplies* a name, "Mr. Simpson," even though a catalogue copy had given the real name, "Mr. Henry Bradbury," as it appears in the original MS, now at the Huntington Library. These and innumerable other examples of garblings that could be cited are a clear indication of how much a scholarly and definitive edition of Dickens's letters is needed.

[40] *Times* Literary Supplement, March 9, 1951, p. 156; this letter is dated August 23, 1858. In the initial period of the separation Miss Coutts, according to Henry Crabb Robinson, had been "satisfied there has been nothing criminal—nothing beyond *incompatibilité d'humeur*," though she deprecated Dickens's "unwise advertisement of domestic calamities" (*Henry Crabb Robinson on Books and Their Writers*, ed. Edith J. Morley, London [1938], II, 778). Robinson's diary entry is dated July 13, 1858; this letter and later developments in Miss Coutts's relations with Dickens offer evidence that the Baroness did not remain satisfied with the explanation of *"incompatibilité d'humeur."*

[41] This probably refers to the annual gathering of the Dickens family with Miss Coutts for the prepublication reading of Dickens's Christmas story for the year, which had become traditional. The reading for the season of 1857 was the story entitled "The Perils of Certain English Prisoners." The domestic tenseness of playing the game of "hiding the skeleton" is indicated in this letter.

[42] *Dickens and Daughter*, p. 107.

[43] *The Letters and Memoirs of Sir William Hardman . . .* Second Series: 1863–1865 (ed., S. M. Ellis), London [1925], p. 148. A year earlier Hardman had referred to Mrs. Dickens as "the wife

from whom the great Charles has so shamefully separated ('discharged with a good character' as Shirley Brooks says of her), and who is a very agreeable lady." (*Ibid.*, p. 8.)

[44] *Letters*, III, 11; the letter is dated March 15, 1858.

[45] *Letters*, III, 14; the first two sentences do not appear in the Nonesuch edition, but are in the original MS at the Morgan library; the letter is dated March 21, 1858.

[46] *Letters*, III, 14.

[47] *Ibid.*, p. 26; the letter is dated June 8, 1858.

[48] *Ibid.*, p. 27.

[49] *Ibid.*, p. 29; dated July 7, 1858.

[50] In a review of the Nonesuch edition of letters, *Saturday Review of Literature*, XIX, 16 (December 24, 1938).

[51] Dated May 31, 1858; MS in the Berg Collection, New York Public Library.

[52] Dated October 23, 1857; original MS in the Berg Collection, New York Public Library. The whole series of unpublished letters to the De la Rues, now in the Berg Collection, reveal Mrs. Dickens's irritation over her husband's great concern about curing Mme. de la Rue's illness through his mesmeric powers, a concern which involved many visits to her at all hours of the day and night.

[53] This letter, as published in the Nonesuch (III, 476), presents a problem. In another portion, Dickens writes: "The 'magic circle' consists of but one member. I don't in the least care for Mrs. T. T. except that her share in the story is (as far as I am concerned) a remembrance impossible to swallow. Therefore, and for the magic sake, I scrupulously try to do her justice, and not to see her—out of my path—with a jaundiced vision." Readers have accepted the Nonesuch editor's identification of "Mrs. T. T." as Mrs. Tom Trollope (i.e., Fanny Ternan), without noting that Fanny did not become Mrs. Trollope until October 29, 1866, whereas the letter is dated July 5, 1866. Since the "magic circle" evidently concerns the Ternans, however, Dickens could easily have meant Mrs. Thomas Ternan, Ellen's mother. The matter is further confused when later in the letter Dickens writes: "Of course you will be very strictly on your guard, if you see Tom Trollope, or his wife, or both,—to make no reference to me which either can piece into anything. She is infinitely sharper than the serpent's Tooth. Mind that." Here Tom is definitely given a wife at a time when he was still a widower. Those who have read the passage as a reference to Fanny Ternan have had to come to the unlikely conclusion that she was in ignorance of her sister's liaison with Dickens. However, there is a good deal of evidence that the members of the Ternan family maintained a strong and intimate relationship with one another. Tom Trollope mentions in his autobiography that it was at first difficult to get Fanny to

come to Italy as governess to his daughter because of her "very strongly-felt family ties." (*What I Remember*, III, 30.) Also, Dickens's letters at this same time about Fanny's first novel, *Aunt Margaret's Trouble* (dedicated to her sister Ellen), reveal a warm and friendly enthusiasm for its author. The reference would apply more aptly to Trollope's first wife, Theodosia, but since she died on April 16, 1865, the only explanation is that this is another misdated or mistranscribed Nonesuch letter. Unfortunately, I have been unable to locate the original.

4. Dickens Speaks

[1] IV, 243–244 (December, 1949).

[2] See Ley's letter to the editor of "Books," New York *Herald Tribune*, July 5, 1936; also his statement in the *Dickensian*, XXXII, 16, and Wagenknecht's in *College English*, XI, 380. Wright's statements appear in the *Life of Charles Dickens*, p. 280, and references to various later "establishments" can be found in other parts of the *Life* and in his autobiography, *Thomas Wright of Olney*. Berger's statement has been quoted above, p. 25.

[3] *Letters*, III, 235. Letter is to Benjamin Webster and is dated September 9, 1861.

[4] Unpublished letter in the Berg Collection, New York Public Library; the name "Fanny" is blacked out on the MS.

[5] First published in T. A. Trollope's *What I Remember*, p. 361.

[6] Spofford later married Harriet Elizabeth Prescott, minor novelist and poet, and daughter of the famous American historian; it was she who gave the letter to the Morgan Library. I have in my possession a letter from Frances Eleanor Trollope to "Cousin Richard" in America asking him to obtain her baptismal certificate from St. Stephen's Church in Philadelphia. The letter is dated from Rome, March 13, 1886.

[7] "The Secret of Dickens' Memoranda," *Bookmen's Holiday: Notes and Studies Written and Gathered in Tribute to Harry Miller Lydenberg* (New York, 1943), 188–195.

[8] The square brackets are in the original MS.

[9] *What I Remember*, III [alternate title, *The Further Reminiscences of Mr. T. A. Trollope*] (London, 1889), p. 92.

[10] *Ibid.*, p. 175.

[11] *Dearest Isa*, pp. 277 f.

[12] *Charles Dickens as Editor: Being Letters Written by Him to William Henry Wills, his Sub-Editor* (London, 1912), p. 367; the original telegram is in the Huntington Library collection.

[13] MS, Morgan Library.

[14] *Letters*, III, 480; the letter is dated August 2, 1866.

¹⁵ I am indebted to Professor Franklin P. Rolfe, who was the first to make these transcriptions, for permission to publish them here.

¹⁶ All MSS quoted here are on deposit at the Huntington Library.

¹⁷ MSS, Huntington Library.

¹⁸ The Huntington Library is in possession of one of the rare copies of *The Frozen Deep*, which was never published but was privately printed in 1866. A narrative version, which differs greatly from the original, was used by Wilkie Collins in his public reading tour in America, and was published in 1874.

5. *Decanonization*

¹ See especially Edmund Wilson, "Dickens: The Two Scrooges," in *The Wound and the Bow: Seven Studies in Literature* (New York, 1941); Lionel Stevenson, "Dickens's Dark Novels, 1851–1857," *Sewanee Review*, LI, 398–409 (1943); and the treatments of Hugh Kingsmill [Lunn], Hesketh Pearson, Jack Lindsay, and Julian Symons in their respective biographies of Dickens.

² *Charles Dickens Fifty Years After* (privately printed by Clement Shorter), June, 1920, p. 1; this volume is a rare reprint (25 copies) of an article which originally appeared in *The Observer*, June 6, 1920.

³ *Letters*, III, 158.

⁴ Unpublished MS, Huntington Library; the letter is dated February 1, 1863.